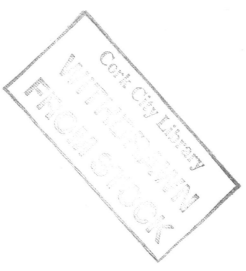

The Christian Heritage

veritas

Desmond Forristal

The Christian Heritage

Veritas Publications Dublin 1976

First published 1976 by
Veritas Publications,
Pranstown House, Booterstown Avenue, Co. Dublin.

© The Irish Episcopal Commission for Catechetics.

This book is part of the Senior Cycle of the Irish Catechetical Programme
prepared by Sr Nano Brennan, Br John Heneghan and Fr Desmond
Forristal.

Designed by Bill Bolger.
Set in 11 on 12 pt Plantin.
Printed and bound in the Republic of Ireland by Cahill (1976) Ltd.,
Dublin.

The author and publishers are grateful to the following for permission to
quote from material on which they hold copyright: Hughes Massie Ltd.:
Poems of St John of the Cross; Burns and Oates: *Works of St John of the
Cross;* Collins Fontana Ltd: Solzhenitsyn, *The First Circle;* Dietrich
Bonhoeffer: *Letters and Papers;* Teilhard de Chardin, (The Preface) *Le
Milieu Divin; Autobiography of a Saint:* The Bodley Head Ltd.:
Solzhenitsyn, *Stories and Prose Poems;* Faber and Faber Ltd.: T. S. Eliot,
Collected Poems 1909-1962; William Heinemann Ltd.: *The Brothers
Karamazov,* Fyodor Dostoevsky; Dent & Sons Ltd.: *Anna Karenina,*
Tolstoy; Penguin Books Ltd.: *The Life of St Teresa* and *The Little Flowers of
St Francis;* Anthony Clarke Books: *Spiritual Exercises of St Ignatius.*

Grateful acknowledgment is also due to the following who gave us
permission to reproduce the subjects illustrated in this book:

Mansell Collection, London: 7, 18, 33, 41 (detail), 46, 56, 62, 67, 68 (detail),
73, 85, 90-91, 99, 104, 106, 107, 122, 123, 125, 127, 129, 131, 132, 134, 143,
148, 149, 154 (2), 155, 158, 160, 163, 168, 176, 177, 179.
Mansell/Anderson: 9, 11, 12, 14, 17, 21, 36, 39, 42 (detail), 89 (detail), 95,
96, 103, 111, 112, 114.
Alinari/Mansell: 13, 26, 31, 35, 54, 71 (detail), 75 (detail), 79, 82, 93, 98,
120.
Commissioners of Public Works in Ireland: 48, 51, 53, 59, 64, 76.
Chester Beatty Library, Dublin: 24.
National Gallery of Ireland: 43, 74.
Trinity College Library, Dublin: 50.
Diocesan Press Office, Dublin: 144.
Camera Press, London: 28, 139, 156, 180, 181, 182.
British Tourist Authority: 170, 171.
National Portrait Gallery, London: 142 (detail), 145.
Trinity College Library, Cambridge: 72.
French Government Tourist Office, London: 65, 66 (detail), 69, 70, 121,
169.
Ciric: 116.
L'Office Central, Lisieux: 151, 152.
Philippe Halsman, New York: 168.
Fr Sean Swayne: 173, 174.
Fr Dermot Clifford: 147.
S. Carty, Enniscorthy: 146.
Fr Joseph Dunn: 101, 128, 130, 132 (3), 137, 143, 153 (2), 167, 185, 187,
189.

Colour illustrations: Alinari, facing pages 32, 65, 128, 129 and 160; Trinity
College, Dublin, facing page 33; Bord Failte, Ireland, facing page 64; Eton
College, England, facing page 161.

ISBN: 0-905092-20-1.

Contents

Colour Plates

CHAPTER ONE

THE PAGAN EMPIRE

The exact date of the birth of Jesus Christ is not known, even though it is the event from which all other events are dated. Every year is numbered by its distance from the birth of Christ. The years before his birth are marked with the letters B.C. (Before Christ) and those after it with the letters A.D. (*Anno Domini*, the year of the Lord).

Our present system of numbering the years was worked out by a monk in Italy called Dionysius Exiguus in the year he called A.D. 525 since he calculated it to be 525 years after the birth of the Lord. He was a little out in his calculations; we now know that King Herod the Great died in 4 B.C. and that Jesus must therefore have been born not later than that. Still the fact remains that every time anyone in the world writes down a date, the birth of Jesus is being used as a standard of reference.

The uncertainty about the exact date of the birth of Jesus is due to the fact that he was born to an unknown family from an insignificant village in a remote province of the Roman Empire. Even his trial and execution, which brought him to the attention of the Roman authorities, were regarded by them as a very minor matter and no record of them survives in the official documents of the time. The death of some seeming religious fanatic in far-off Jerusalem was not a thing to cause any disturbance in the smooth-running machinery of the Roman Empire.

A Roman ship. This ancient Roman painting shows dockers loading a cargo ship with sacks of grain.

During that period, the first century of the Christian era, the Roman Empire was at the height of its power. The Mediterranean Sea and all the lands that touched it were Roman. To the north its frontier was the two great rivers, the Rhine and the Danube. To the south it took in the coastland of Africa from the sea to the desert. In the east it included Asia Minor (modern Turkey), Syria, Palestine, and Egypt. From the Atlantic to the Black Sea hundreds of millions of people enjoyed the benefits of Roman rule and Roman civilisation; and the chief of these benefits was the Roman peace, the *Pax Romana*.

Never before and never since have so many people enjoyed peace for so long a time. The Roman armies continued as a fighting force but their fighting was done at the frontiers: fending off the barbarians from northern Europe and guarding the eastern outposts against the Persian Empire. Inside the Roman borders there was peace. Trade and agriculture flourished, literature and the arts were cultivated, laws were made and justice was administered. Roman towns were built everywhere to an almost identical plan, each with its central square or forum, its law-court, its temple and its theatre, each watered by a Roman aqueduct and linked by a Roman road to its nearest neighbour.

Communication was quick and easy. The Roman roads could be used in all weathers on foot or on horseback and the traveller had little to fear from bandits or pirates. Ships crossed the Mediterranean Sea from one well-equipped port to another. There were no borders, no customs examinations, no passports. There was a safe and efficient postal service between the different cities and provinces.

The Romans were keen letter-writers. Since there was no printing there were no newspapers: but news travelled quickly in the form of letters which were often read aloud to groups. The ability to read and write was widespread. Latin was the official language of the Empire but in Greece, Egypt and the East, Greek was more generally spoken. In Italy and the West, Latin was the language of ordinary speech though most educated people spoke both languages. Even in the city of Rome itself, cultured people liked to show off their knowledge of Greek, the language of the great poets and dramatists; but this was partly snobbery, since the great age of Greek literature was long past and the best writers were now using Latin.

From the worldly point of view, the Empire was a remarkably impressive achievement; but from the spiritual point of view, it left much to be desired.

Various types of gladiators are shown in action in this ancient Roman mosaic.

Roman religion was no more than a collection of superstitions, combining gods from Italy, Greece, Egypt and elsewhere. Only a few philosophers had any concept of a single supreme God. For most people, religion was a matter of guarding against misfortune by offering prayers and sacrifices to a variety of divine and semi-divine figures, among whom the Emperor himself was included.

There was no connection in the average person's mind between religion and morality. The traditional Roman virtues of honesty, sobriety and industry fell into disregard as the Empire and its people grew richer. Sexual morality became lax, marriage was little respected, and some of the pagan temples themselves were centres of drunkenness and prostitution.

The Roman vice that shocks us most today, however, is none of these. It is their cruelty. Crucifixion was only one of the many methods of torture and execution to which people were condemned for comparatively light offences. Romans enjoyed the sight of human suffering and on public holidays gladiators fought to the death against one another or against wild beasts in order to entertain the public. The theatres fell out of favour and the arenas grew in popularity, putting on ever more cruel and bloody spectacles to satisfy their audiences.

The First Christians
This was the world in which Jesus lived and died. His particular corner of that world had one peculiarity of its own. Palestine was the home of the Jewish religion, the only religion which worshipped a single God, rejected idols and upheld a high standard of morality. It also had links with many other parts of the Roman world through the Jews of the *Diaspora* (a Greek word meaning dispersion) who had left their homeland in search of work and brought their religion with them.

The day of Pentecost, when St Peter preached to the

9

Jews in Jerusalem and three thousand people were baptised, is generally regarded as the day when the Christian Church was founded. At first it was looked upon as a branch of the Jewish religion and the first Christian missionaries were all Jews who brought the good news of the coming of the Messiah to their fellow Jews in different parts of the world. The ease of travel throughout the Empire made the task of these missionaries much easier than it would otherwise have been.

Among them, the outstanding figure is St Paul. As well as being a great saint and a great missionary, he was to become the first great Christian writer. In each city he visited he started a community of believers, both Jews and Gentiles, and kept in touch with them afterwards by means of letters of striking eloquence and insight. These letters, written in Greek, were read and read again by the people to whom they were addressed, and copies were made and sent to be read in other cities. Some of the other apostles also wrote letters which have survived, while at the same time collections were being made of the sayings and doings of Jesus which were to form the basis of the four Gospels.

Thirty years after the death of Jesus, the new religion had communities of believers, called "churches", in many places. The city of Rome had its church, under the leadership of St Peter himself. The collection of writings which was to form the *New Testament* was being built up. The Christians were starting to attract attention, not all of it favourable. Their condemnation of pagan morals, their refusal to honour the gods, their worship of a criminal executed by Rome, made people look upon them with suspicion. The stage was being set for a clash between the old way of life and the new.

In the year 64 a large part of the city of Rome was destroyed by a fire. The rumour went around that the fire had been started at the command of the Emperor Nero in order to clear the way for new buildings; it was even said that the half-crazy tyrant had been seen singing and playing the lyre as he watched the city go up in flames. To avoid the danger of an uprising, Nero decided to put the blame somewhere else. What happened next is described by the pagan writer, Tacitus, who was probably an eye-witness of these events:

> To stop these rumours, Nero put the blame on a class of people who are hated for their abominations, commonly known as Christians, and punished them

with the utmost cruelty.

They get their name from Christ, who was executed by Pontius Pilate in the reign of Tiberius. Despite this temporary setback, this pernicious superstition broke out again, not just in Judaea, the source of the evil, but even in Rome, that sink where anything foul and degrading from any part of the world is sure to find a following.

This statue of St Peter was made many centuries after his death but is probably based on earlier portraits or descriptions. It is now in St Peter's in Rome.

11

The Emperor Nero. He committed suicide at the age of 30 when the people rebelled against his tyranny.

The first to be arrested were some who had confessed. Then, on their evidence, a huge number were judged guilty, not so much of causing the fire as of hating the human race. These were not merely put to death, they were also made to serve as objects of amusement. Some were dressed in the skins of animals and torn to death by dogs; some were crucified; some were set on fire in order to light up the darkness after nightfall. Nero opened his gardens to the public for the occasion and put on a show in the circus, where he went among the people dressed as a charioteer and drove around in his chariot. The result was to arouse pity for these men, even though they deserved the severest punishment; because it was felt that they were being destroyed not for the general good but to satisfy the cruel instincts of one man.

Among those who died during Nero's persecution were Peter, who was crucified, and Paul, who was beheaded. Nero himself committed suicide in 68 but his laws against the Christians remained in force. For two and a half centuries the penalty for being a Christian in the Roman Empire was death.

In spite of this, the new religion continued to spread. The laws against it were often not enforced and there were times and places where Christians could practise their faith openly. But people continued to believe them guilty of all kinds of abominations, of incest, of cannibalism, of hating the human race. A Christian could be informed on at any time and brought before the courts, where he had to choose between apostasy and death.

Half a century after Nero's persecution, Pliny, the Governor of Bithynia on the Black Sea, found himself conducting his own persecution of the Christians as a result of an anonymous pamphlet which accused a number of his subjects by name. He wrote to the Emperor to ask his advice and both his letter and the Emperor's reply have been preserved. In the course of his letter, Pliny said:

> I released all those who denied they were Christians, because they agreed to invoke the gods, to pay homage with incense and wine to your image when I had it brought out along with the statues of the gods, and above all because they cursed Christ, which it is said no real Christian can ever be induced to do.
>
> Others who were named by the informer first admitted being Christians and then denied it, saying they had been once but not any longer; some had recanted three or more years ago, one or two as

much as twenty years ago. They all worshipped your image and the statues of the gods and cursed Christ.

They said however that all they had ever done was this. They used to meet before daybreak on an appointed day and recite a hymn in turn to Christ as if he were a god; and they used to bind themselves under oath not for any criminal purpose but to avoid theft, robbery, adultery, breach of faith, and failing to return a loan. After this ceremony, they used to go home but they would come back later to have a meal together; but the food was ordinary, harmless food, and they had stopped meeting for this meal after I issued my edict banning secret societies in accordance with your instructions.

The Governor ended by asking what he was to do about the Christians; without saying it in so many words, he clearly felt unhappy about putting to death people whose only crime was their religious beliefs. Trajan, the Emperor, in his reply suggested what he felt to be the best way to deal with the Christians:

The Emperor Trajan, who ordered that Christians should not be sought out but must be punished if found.

They are not to be sought out. If they are informed against and the charge is proved, they are to be punished. However, if anyone denies he is a Christian and proves it by worshipping our gods, he is to be automatically acquitted no matter how suspicious his behaviour may have been in the past. Anonymous pamphlets should never be admitted as evidence. They are a very bad precedent and out of keeping with modern times.

Trajan, one of the best of the Roman emperors, still was not prepared to repeal the laws against Christians. He may have been wise enough to see that the Christians were a threat to his idea of the Empire, that they were loyal to Caesar only as long as this did not conflict with their loyalty towards God.

The Early Church

By the middle of the second century, the Christians were beginning to defend themselves against their enemies. Christian writers were setting down what they believed and showing how untrue were the accusations made against them. The writers of these early times are of great importance, since they bear witness to the beliefs of the first Christians and are close in time to the apostles and to Jesus himself. The main writers of the first six centuries or so are generally known as the Fathers of the Church, because of the part they played in shaping the life and thought of the Christian Church.

The first great Christian writer was the philosopher

13

Justin (c.100 — c.165). Born in Palestine, he spent the first thirty years of his life searching for truth among the various philosophies of the time and finally found that truth in Christianity. Among the works he wrote in defence of his new religion was his *Apologia*, addressed to the Emperor Antoninus Pius: the word *apologia* is the Greek for "defence" and for this reason Justin and the other early defenders of Christianity are sometimes called the Apologists. Justin's *Apologia* still

An early anti-Christian wall-drawing found in Rome. The Greek inscription reads: "Alaxamenos adores his God".

survives (along with his *Dialogue with Tryphon* and a second, shorter *Apologia*) and it is the first work of Christian theology that we have, even though it was meant to be read by unbelievers rather than by believers. In order to answer the false accusations, he has to describe Christian belief and practice in detail and show how innocent and indeed elevated they are. He himself was arrested and beheaded in Rome about the year 165 but his writings lived on.

One of the most interesting parts of his *Apologia* deals with the eucharist. "We are taught," he writes, "that the food over which the prayer of thanksgiving containing his words has been said, the food which nourishes and is absorbed into our own flesh and blood, is the flesh and blood of this Jesus who became flesh." He goes on to describe the Sunday eucharist in Rome about the year 150:

> On that day which is named after the sun, all who are in the towns and in the country gather together for a communal celebration. And then the memoirs of the apostles or the writings of the prophets are read, as long as time permits. After the reader has finished, the one presiding gives an address, urgently exhorting his hearers to practise these beautiful teachings in their lives. Then all stand up together and recite prayers. After the prayers are over, as has already been remarked, the bread and wine mixed with water are brought forward, and the president offers up prayers and thanksgivings, as much as in him lies. The people join in with an "Amen". Then takes place the distribution to all those present of the things over which the thanksgiving had been spoken. The deacons bring a portion to those who are absent. Moreover, those who are well-off give whatever they will; what is collected is left with the president, who uses it to help orphans and widows, those in want owing to sickness or any other cause, prisoners, travellers, and in short anyone who is in any need.

This is the first detailed description the pagan world had of the Christian eucharist, that rite which Pliny had tried to describe from his conversations with Christian sympathisers some forty years before. In Justin's description the main features of the Mass are already present: the readings from the Old and New Testaments, the offering of bread and wine, the words of consecration (given by Justin in another part of the book), the distribution of Holy Communion, even the collection.

The writings of St Justin and the other apologists

tell us much about the early Church: but since they were written for outsiders, they do not tell us everything. To fill in some of the gaps, we have letters written by Christians to one another during those times. One of the earliest and most important of these is the letter written about the year 95 by St Clement, Bishop of Rome, to the Christians of Corinth in Greece. Its object was to settle a dispute which had arisen in the Church in Corinth. Although the title of Pope had not yet been applied to the Bishop of Rome, the letter shows clearly that even in those early days his authority was respected far outside Rome itself.

Other early letters which survive are the seven written by St Ignatius, Bishop of Antioch, who was taken to Rome to be martyred about 107. From them we can see the important part the local bishop played in guiding and uniting the local Christian community. "Do nothing without the bishop," he wrote, "keep your body as the temple of God, love unity, flee from divisions, be imitators of Jesus Christ, as he was imitator of the Father."

St Irenaeus, who came from Smyrna in Asia Minor, was the first great theologian. He left Smyrna as a young man and went to live at Lyons in France; and when the Bishop of Lyons was martyred in 177, Irenaeus was chosen as the new bishop. It was there that he wrote his book *Against the Heresies*, which for the first time set out the main truths of Christianity in connected and logical order. He argued against those heretics who were introducing new doctrines because they were departing from the traditional faith of the churches and particularly the faith of the Church of Rome, with which all other churches should agree. He died about 202, possibly by martyrdom.

The fact that this first work of Christian theology was written in France shows how Christianity was spreading throughout Europe in spite of savage persecution. It was also spreading in North Africa and most of the important Christian writers of the hundred years after Irenaeus came from that area. In Egypt, the city of Alexandria became a centre of theology and included among its leading writers Clement of Alexandria and his pupil, Origen.

Further west, in that region which we call Tunisia and Algeria but which the Romans simply called Africa, there were Tertullian, the first Christian writer to use the Latin rather than the Greek language, and St Cyprian, the great Bishop of Carthage. In spite of the terrible times in which they lived, these men continued to give witness to the faith even at the risk of their lives.

St Cyprian's last work was a short book of encouragement for those facing martyrdom; shortly after finishing it, he was himself arrested and beheaded, in the year 258.

Even with all these writings to help us, it is not easy to imagine the life of the early Church. The very word "church" itself may mislead us. When the early Christians used the word church *(ecclesia)*, they meant the community of believers; either the entire community of believers throughout the world, or else the community in a given place — the church at Rome, the church at Lyons, the church at Carthage, and so on.

Churches in the sense of church buildings did not exist and could not exist as long as the Christians were a hunted, hidden sect. When they met for their eucharist, they met in a room in a private house. The altar was a table, the priest's vestments were his ordinary clothes. Anything that could arouse the

MVNIFICENTIA LEONIS. XIII. P. M.

suspicions of the authorities had to be avoided. The room must look like an ordinary room when the ceremony was over.

A third-century sarcophagus. A pagan would probably not realise that the figure in the centre represented Christ, the good shepherd.

This is why we have little in the way of Christian art from the first three centuries. A picture or a statue could lead to torture and death if seen by the wrong eyes. Obvious signs of Christianity like the cross were kept out of sight. Instead, the Christians often had pictures or carvings which appeared harmless to the unbeliever but had a special meaning for the believer. A young man with a sheep on his shoulders stood for the Good Shepherd. A man or woman with hands raised up signified prayer and union with God. A fish stood for Christ the saviour, since the initial letters of the Greek phrase "Jesus Christ, Son of God, Saviour" made up the Greek word for a fish.

A painting of loaves and a fish from the Roman catacombs.

There were occasional times and places when Christians felt safe in depicting their beliefs more openly. One such place was Dura Europos, a small town on the very furthest eastern edge of the Roman Empire. In 1931 the remains of a house were found there which was decorated with religious paintings and which had obviously been used for baptism and the eucharist. The house had been built some time before 250 and is the nearest thing to a church building that we have from all this period.

Early Christian paintings are also found in Rome on the walls and ceilings of the catacombs, which were underground burial places. A dead man could not be punished for his beliefs, so it was safe to have a religious emblem drawn over his grave or carved on his sarcophagus (a kind of stone coffin).

Most of the scenes shown in Dura Europos and in the catacombs came from the Bible and they were usually chosen so as to remind the onlooker that Christ saved him from sin through baptism. Adam and Eve, Moses drawing water from the rock, Jonah saved from the whale, Daniel preserved from the lions, the three young men rescued from the fiery furnace, were among the most common subjects. Scenes from the life of Jesus were less common and the crucifixion was never shown, perhaps from a sense of reverence: indeed, the only drawing of the crucifixion we have from this period is an insulting one drawn by a pagan and showing Christ with the body of a man and the head of a donkey. But Christ is shown as a child with his mother, being baptised in the Jordan, curing the sick, and as the Good Shepherd.

These early images of Christ are of no value as

18

likenesses. They were obviously not meant to portray him as he really was, since they generally show him as a Roman rather than a Jew, dressed in Roman clothes, cleanshaven and shorthaired in the Roman style. The artistic value of these and the other biblical scenes is also slight; both the drawing and the carving is generally crude and second-rate.

Yet with all their faults, these first beginnings of Christian art are very precious. They show the signs of having been made furtively and hastily, with poor materials and inferior craftsmanship, but they still have the power to move us deeply. Their very roughness reminds us of the troubled times in which they were made and of the faith and courage of those who made them.

Building up the Faith

The building of churches of stone had to wait until the end of persecution. The building of churches in the other sense of the word, that is, communities of believers, went on all the time. The centre of the life of the Church was, as we have seen, the eucharist; but before the new converts were admitted to the eucharist, they had to go through a period of preparation.

The number of converts continued to grow in every part of the Empire. The best people in every walk of life found themselves drawn by the personality of Jesus and the nobility of his teaching, just as they found themselves sickened by the cruelty and permissiveness of pagan life. In particular they were impressed by the extraordinary bravery of the martyrs. Men, women and children went joyfully to meet death in the arena. The laws against the new religion had the opposite effect to what was intended, as Tertullian pointed out:

> Crucify us, torture us, condemn us, grind us into dust ... The more you cut us down, the more we grow. The blood of Christians is a seed.

During the time of preparation, the convert was called a catechumen, a Greek word meaning learner. The catechumen attended a series of instructions on the Apostles' Creed, on Christian morality, and on prayer. He or she was allowed to be present at the readings and homily which formed the first part of the Sunday service; but only the baptised could remain on for the eucharist itself.

Baptism was usually given during the Easter vigil, the night when Jesus arose from the dead. When possible it took place in a spring or river of flowing water, and the catechumens were immersed three

19

times. After that they were anointed with oil, dressed in white robes and fed with milk and honey, the food of new-born infants. Then for the first time these new Christians joined their brothers and sisters in the faith to celebrate the eucharist and receive the body and blood of the Lord.

From then on they took their full part in the life of their local church. Each church was ruled by a bishop, with the help of a number of priests and deacons. These were elected by the members of the local church and ordained by the laying on of hands, and they were usually married men who had ordinary jobs and carried out their ministry in their spare time. Women also played a large part in the life of the community and there are many references to the good work done by deaconesses and widows.

The centre of the Christian's life was, as we have seen, the eucharist. Every Sunday, the day of the Resurrection, was a holy day, though Easter Sunday and Pentecost Sunday were given special honour. At their Sunday meetings, the Christians strengthened and encouraged one another, and listened to readings which included letters from other churches and stories of the martyrs, as well as passages from the scriptures. Then followed the celebration of the Lord's Supper. The faithful, who had already shown their love for one another by exchanging the kiss of peace, now cemented that love by sharing in the same spiritual food and drink. As they stood around the holy table, their hands held high in the attitude of prayer, they felt in themselves that strength and union with God which would sustain them in the days to come. In the words of Clement of Alexandria:

> Our heads uplifted, our arms raised to heaven, even when the spoken prayer is ended we remain drawn towards the spiritual world in the unseen vibrations of our souls. The Christian is praying while he walks, while he talks, while he rests, while he works or reads; and when he meditates alone in the secret retreat of his own soul and calls upon the Father with sighs that are no less real because they are unvoiced, the Father never fails to answer and to draw close to him.

In theory, the new Christians had been freed from sin by baptism and from then on lived a life of prayer and holiness. In practice, they were still human and sometimes fell again into sin. Three sins were regarded as specially serious: idolatry, murder and adultery. Sinners who repented were absolved by the bishop or

priest but often had to do public penance for years before being admitted again to Holy Communion. The rules about absolution from sins varied from place to place and sometimes gave rise to heated controversy. Tertullian, who held some very extreme views, said that the three capital sins could never be absolved by the Church but only by God.

The ruins of the Colosseum in Rome. Other Roman cities also had amphitheatres where gladiators fought to the death and Christians were exposed to wild animals.

Martyrs and Miracles

Among the most treasured possessions of the early Christians were their books. First and foremost, there were the Four Gospels and the other writings of the New Testament. These were copied in large numbers and circulated throughout the Empire. They were quickly translated into Latin for those who did not understand Greek. The writings of the Old Testament were also held in great reverence and Latin translations of these soon followed.

The better-educated Christians could deepen their understanding of their faith by reading the works of such men as Irenaeus, Tertullian, Clement and Origen. But the majority of Christians were poor people, tradesmen, labourers, slaves, who preferred to read (or, if they could not read, listen to) heroic stories of the sufferings and deaths of the martyrs.

Some of these stories were taken from the official records of the court proceedings, others were based on

21

eye-witness reports of the martyrs' last hours. A good example of the first kind is the account of the trial of St Justin and a number of others in Rome about the year 165:

> The prefect Rusticus said: 'Do you think, then, that you will ascend to heaven to receive a fitting reward?'
>
> 'I do not think,' said Justin. 'I have definite knowledge and am fully certain of it.'
>
> 'Well then,' said the prefect Rusticus, 'let us come to the point at issue, the thing that must be settled. Will you agree to offer sacrifice to the gods?'
>
> 'No one in his right mind turns from piety to impiety,' said Justin.
>
> The prefect Rusticus said: 'If you do not obey, you will be punished without mercy.'
>
> Justin said: 'We are confident that if we suffer this penalty for the sake of our Lord Jesus Christ we shall be saved; this is the confidence and salvation we shall have at the terrible tribunal of our saviour and master, sitting in judgment over the whole world.'
>
> Similarly the other martyrs said: 'Do what you will. We are Christians and we do not offer sacrifice to idols.'
>
> Then the prefect Rusticus passed judgment, saying: 'Those who have refused to sacrifice to the gods and to obey the Emperor's edict are to be led away to be scourged and beheaded in accordance with the law.'

An example of the second kind is the story of the martyrdom of Perpetua and Felicity in Africa about 203, which may well have been written by Tertullian. Perpetua was the mother of a young baby and Felicity was advanced in pregnancy when they were sentenced to death, along with a number of other Christians. Felicity was worried that her execution might be delayed on account of her condition: she wanted to die with her fellow Christians and not with common criminals. So all the prisoners joined together to pray for the birth of her baby:

> As soon as they had finished praying, her labour began. She suffered a good deal during the birth because of the difficulty of her eight months' delivery.
>
> Seeing this, one of the assistant jailers said to her: 'You are suffering now, but what will you do when you are thrown to the beasts? Little did you think of that when you refused to sacrifice.'
>
> 'What I am suffering now,' she answered, 'I am

suffering by myself. But then I will have someone within me, and he will suffer for me just as I will suffer for him.'

She gave birth to a girl, and one of the sisters brought her up as her own daughter.

The story goes on to describe the death of the two women. They were exposed in the arena to a wild heifer, which tossed them but did not kill them. Then they were put to the sword. Perpetua herself had to guide the trembling hand of the young gladiator who was ordered to kill her.

It is easy to imagine the effect stories of this kind had on the first Christians: even today they have not lost the power to move us. But, as happens in every age, there were those who hungered for something more dramatic and sensational. To meet this hunger, fantastic legends were manufactured in which spotless maidens confront villainous judges and go to their deaths accompanied by spectacular miracles. When a young man tries to lay hands on St Agnes, he is struck by lightning. When St Catherine is tied to a spiked wheel, the wheel flies apart and kills half the spectators. There were no doubt a real Agnes, Catherine, Lucy, Cecilia, but the accounts of their deaths that have come down to us bear all the signs of being pious fictions. Though they compare very unfavourably with the sincerity and restraint of the true accounts, these legends were very popular in their own time and long afterwards.

The same misguided talent for invention was applied to the Gospels. People had a natural curiosity about the life of Jesus and his mother and wanted to know more about these parts of their lives, especially their early lives, which were not described in the Four Gospels. Apocryphal gospels were written to fill in the gaps and were attributed to various apostles. They were often as far-fetched as the legends of the martyrs and they became equally popular among the sensation-seekers.

The *Infancy Gospel of St Thomas* tells of various marvels performed by Jesus as a boy. Some of these are petty and pointless, others are downright vicious. In one incident, the five-year-old Jesus models twelve sparrows out of clay on the Sabbath; when Joseph rebukes him, he claps his hands and the birds come to life and fly away chirping. In another incident, a child bumps against Jesus who threatens him: "You shall not go further on your way." The child is at once struck down by a mysterious ailment until Jesus consents to cure him.

Here and there these forgeries may contain scraps of

ΔΕϹΜΙΩΝ ΩϹ ϹΥΝΔΕΔΕΜΕΝΟΙ ΤΩΝ ΚΑ
ΚΟΥΧΟΥΜΕΝΩΝ ΩϹ ΚΑΙ ΑΥΤΟΙ ΟΝΤΕϹ ΕΝ
ϹΩΜΑΤΙ ΤΙΜΙΟϹ Ο ΓΑΜΟϹ ΕΝ ΠΑϹΙΝ ΚΑΙ
Η ΚΟΙΤΗ ΑΜΙΑΝΤΟϹ ΠΟΡΝΟΥϹ ΓΑΡ ΚΑΙ
ΜΟΙΧΟΥϹ ΚΡΙΝΕΙ Ο ΘΕ ΑΦΙΛΑΡΓΥ
ΡΟϹ Ο ΤΡΟΠΟϹ ΑΡΚΟΥΜΕΝΟΙ ΤΟΙϹ ΠΑΡΟΥ
ϹΙΝ ΑΥΤΟϹ ΓΑΡ ΕΙΡΗΚΕΝ ΟΥ ΜΗ ϹΕ ΑΝΩ
ΟΥΔ ΟΥ ΜΗ ϹΕ ΕΝΚΑΤΑΛΕΙΠΩ ΩϹΤΕ
ΘΑΡΡΟΥΝΤΑϹ ΛΕΓΕΙΝ ΚϹ ΕΜΟΙ
ΚΑΙ ΟΥ ΦΟΒΗΘΗϹΟΜΑΙ ΤΙ ΠΟΙΗϹΕΙ
ΑΝΘΡΩΠΟϹ ΜΝΗΜΟΝΕΥΕΤΕ ΤΩΝ
ΗΓΟΥΜΕΝΩΝ ΟΙΤΙΝΕϹ ΕΛΑΛΗϹΑΝ
ΥΜΕΙΝ ΤΟΝ ΛΟΓΟΝ ΤΟΥ ΘΥ ΩΝ ΑΝΑ
ΘΕΩΡΟΥΝΤΕϹ ΤΗΝ ΕΚΒΑϹΙΝ ΤΗϹ
ΑΝΑϹΤΡΟΦΗϹ ΜΕΙΜΕΙϹΘΕ ΤΗΝ
ΠΙϹΤΙΝ ΙΗϹ ΧΡϹ ΕΧΘΕϹ ΚΑΙ ϹΗΜΕΡΟΝ
Ο ΑΥΤΟϹ ΚΑΙ ΕΙϹ ΤΟΥϹ ΑΙΩΝΑϹ ΔΙΔΑΧΑΙϹ
ΠΟΙΚΙΛΑΙϹ ΚΑΙ ΞΕΝΑΙϹ ΜΗ ΠΑΡΑ
ΦΕΡΕϹΘΕ ΚΑΛΟΝ ΓΑΡ ΧΑΡΙΤΙ ΒΕΒΑΙΟΥ
ϹΘΑΙ ΤΗΝ ΚΑΡΔΙΑΝ ΟΥ ΒΡΩΜΑϹΙΝ ΕΝ ΟΙϹ ΟΥΚ
ΩΦΕΛΗΘΗϹΑΝ ΟΙ ΠΕΡΙΠΑΤΟΥΝΤΕϹ
ΕΧΟΜΕΝ ΘΥϹΙΑϹΤΗΡΙΟΝ ΕΞ ΟΥ
ΟΥΚ ΕΧΟΥϹΙΝ ΕΞΟΥϹΙΑΝ ΟΙ ΤΗ
ϹΚΗΝΗ ΛΑΤΡΕΥΟΝΤΕϹ ΩΝ ΕΙϹΦΕ
ΖΩΩΝ ΤΟ ΑΙΜΑ ΠΕΡΙ ΑΜΑΡ
ΕΙϹ ΤΑ ΑΓΙΑ

genuine information. The *Gospel of St James* gives the names of Mary's parents as Joachim and Anne, and these names have been accepted by the Church. They also contain some impressive passages. The account of the Resurrection in the *Gospel of St Peter* ends with a strange haunting power in spite of all its sensationalism:

> Now in the night when the Lord's day dawned, while the soldiers were taking turns two by two to mount guard, there was a loud noise in the heavens. They saw the heavens opened and two men, shining with light, coming down and approaching the tomb. The stone which had been placed over the doorway rolled away to one side of its own accord. The tomb was opened and the two young men went into it.
>
> On seeing this, the soldiers wakened the centurion and the elders who were also there keeping guard. While they were relating what they had seen, they now beheld three men coming out of the tomb, two of them supporting the other, and a cross following them. And the head of those two reached the sky but the head of him they led over-topped the heavens.

These and other writings attributed to the apostles were widely read and distributed. But the Church, wiser than individual Christians, refused to accept them as the inspired work of God and they gradually faded away and were forgotten.

Left:
This piece of papyrus, dating from the 2nd century, contains part of one of St Paul's letters. It is now in the Chester Beatty Library in Dublin.

CHAPTER TWO

THE CHRISTIAN EMPIRE

In the year 313 the long night of persecution finally came to an end. The so-called Edict of Milan put an end to the laws against Christians and guaranteed freedom of religion for all throughout the Empire.

This was not something that had come about by a slow and peaceful process. On the contrary, the ten years leading up to it saw one of the most violent and widespread of all the persecutions. It was begun by the Emperor Diocletian in 303 and carried on by his successor Galerius. Citizens were ordered to prove their loyalty by placing a few grains of incense in an incense-burner before a pagan statue; those who refused were liable to torture and death. Many Christians suffered in this persecution, especially in the eastern part of the Empire, but their number had now become so large and they had so many sympathisers among the rest of the population that the attempt to destroy them was a complete failure and ended by plunging the whole Roman world into chaos.

From this chaos emerged the man who was to become the first Christian emperor. His name was Constantine and he was the son of one of Diocletian's assistant emperors. Through all the turbulence of the time (at one stage there were no less than seven rival emperors battling one another) Constantine fought to the top and by 312 was strong enough to lead his army against Rome itself.

Encamped outside the city the night before the decisive battle, Constantine had a dream. He himself seems to have given different accounts of this dream, accounts that became more elaborate as he grew older: but the gist of the message he received was that he was to put the sign of the true God upon his soldiers' shields before going into battle. Though he was not a Christian at the time, he was sympathetic to their

The central panel on this 4th century sarcophagus from Rome shows the soldiers guarding the tomb of Christ, and the cross surmounted by the chi-rho sign. The other panels show (left to right) Simon carrying the cross, the crowning with thorns, Jesus guarded by a soldier and Pilate washing his hands.

religion and this dream turned sympathy into belief. The next day he went into battle as one committed to the cause of Christ and won the victory that made him master of Rome. The following year at Milan he issued the edict which gave Christians for the first time full equality before the law.

The sign which Constantine's soldiers put on their shields was not a simple sign of the cross. It was what is called the *chi-rho* sign, made up of the first two letters of the name of Christ in Greek: X (called *Chi*) is the Greek ch, and P (called *rho*) is the Greek r. These two letters were combined into a single monogram in which the X by its shape symbolized the cross as well as the name of Christ; sometimes the X was placed on its side to show the resemblance to the cross more clearly.

Constantine had understandably an almost superstitious reverence for this sign and he ordered it to be put on the banner of the army and the coins of the Empire, and soon it was everywhere to be seen. It has remained one of the most widespread of all Christian symbols and is still found in churches, carved in wood or stone, set in stained glass, embroidered on vestments.

The next hundred years were to prove a golden age in the history of the Church. All the pent-up energy of the previous centuries was suddenly released and there was a marvellous flowering of art, of architecture, of writing, of spirituality, a joyous exploring of all the possibilities of human life in the light of the Christian message.

No one entered into all this more wholeheartedly than the Emperor Constantine himself. For twenty-five years, until his death in 337, he considered himself the ruler of the Church as well as of the Empire, a benevolent despot whose every wish had to be obeyed. Following a custom which was regrettably common at the time, he postponed his baptism until he was on his deathbed. There were a number of crimes which he wanted to commit and he did not fancy having to perform long penances for them: among these were the murder of anyone who aroused his jealousy, including his eldest son and his wife. His memory has always been held in affection by the Church as a man of many great qualities, but a movement to have him declared a saint after his death did not prove very successful.

One of his most important actions was his decision to move the capital of the Empire from Rome in the west to Byzantium in the east. He changed the name Byzantium to Constantinople, the city of Constantine, and there he reigned amid the jewels and ceremony

St Catherine's monastery in the desert of Sinai is one of the oldest in the world. This is the kind of wilderness in which the desert fathers lived.

that have come to be associated with the word Byzantine. One effect of this was to widen the gap between the Greek-speaking east and the Latin-speaking west. The western Christians tended to look to the Bishop of Rome for guidance, the eastern Christians to the Bishop of Constantinople. Another effect was the eventual overrunning of the west by the barbarians: when the frontiers of the Empire crumbled before them like dykes before a flood, the best troops were kept to defend the area around Constantinople and the west was left to its fate.

The Writings of the Fathers

All this lay far in the future in those heady days after the Edict of Milan. At this stage the Christians were still a minority in the Empire, but their numbers were growing very rapidly. The new religion was still largely confined to the towns: the conservative countryfolk were slow to leave their old beliefs. The intellectuals were also hard to win over and for a long time it was fashionable among them to despise the Christians as socially inferior and to make unfavourable comparisons between the simplicity of the Gospels and the polish of the great classical writers.

Yet it was from these sophisticated circles that the new religion was to draw its most distinguished thinkers and writers, those men who are generally grouped together as the Fathers of the fourth century. Though they grew up in widely scattered parts of the Empire, their lives followed a remarkably similar pattern. They were all born to educated parents, with the mother if not the father a Christian, they all studied for many years under the best pagan teachers of the day but were nonetheless irresistibly drawn to seek baptism into the Church. As Christians, and later on as priests and bishops, they devoted their talents to the faith, deepening and developing the Church's understanding of the message brought by Jesus and correcting the errors and heresies of the time.

Errors and heresies were not something new in the Church but they became more noticeable now that Christians had come out into the open. Most of these heresies concerned the nature of the Trinity and the relation between the divine and the human in Jesus, difficult and profound matters in which even the wisest could go astray. To settle these disputes, the custom arose of calling together general councils of the Church, attended by bishops from all over the world. The first of these was the Council of Nicaea in Asia Minor, which was held at the command of Constantine in 325 to discuss the teachings of Arius: the Emperor himself insisted on contributing to the debates, though not even baptised at the time. The Council condemned the view of Arius that the Son was subordinate to the Father, the view that afterwards became known as Arianism.

This was not the end of the matter. Arianism continued to flourish for a long time, along with other heresies, and it was to defend the true Catholic faith against their attacks that the Fathers of this period wrote most of their books. Among those who wrote in Greek were St Athanasius, Bishop of Alexandria, who

was many times driven from his city by the hatred of the Arians; St John Chrysostom, Bishop of Constantinople and the most eloquent preacher of his time; and the three bishops who came from Cappadocia in Asia Minor, St Basil of Caesarea, St Gregory of Nazianzus and St Gregory of Nyssa.

Those who wrote in Latin included St Ambrose, Bishop of Milan and author of some of the first Latin hymns; his disciple and admirer St Augustine, Bishop of Hippo in Africa; and St Jerome, the greatest biblical scholar of his day. Jerome, the only one of these who did not become a bishop, learnt both Greek and Hebrew and translated the whole Bible into Latin; his translation, known as the Vulgate, became and remained the standard version of the Bible.

Among these great names, the greatest is that of Augustine (354-430). He stands out, not only among the Fathers but among all the writers of the ancient world, as someone we can understand and feel for. Like that other talented African, Tertullian, he was sometimes extreme in his views: his gloomy teaching on predestination and on the fate of unbaptised infants finds few supporters today. What he is best remembered for today is the book which he called his *Confessions* and in which he opened his heart as no one had ever done before and few have done since.

By confessions Augustine did not mean confessions of his past sins (though these are included) but confessions of his faith in God. The whole book is addressed to God and it bears the signs of having been written quickly: not because it is badly written but because it moves with an extraordinary rush of energy. It is as full of quotable sayings as *Hamlet*. The very first page sums up his whole life in one unforgettable phrase:"you have made us for yourself and our hearts can never rest until they rest in you."

He tells us that his mother, Monica, was a Christian; but he was not baptised as a child and as he grew older he drifted away from her good influence. Before he was twenty he had adopted a completely pagan way of life and was living with a girl who had borne him a son. Still his mother never stopped hoping and praying for his conversion.

His outstanding ability as a teacher brought him to Carthage, then Rome, then Milan, but no matter how far he travelled he could not shake off the conviction that the God of the Christians was the true God. He tried every other religion and philosophy but none of them satisfied him. The more he struggled to escape from Christianity, the more he became convinced of its truth. At length the only thing that held him back was his unwillingness to change his pagan way of life and obey the moral law. "Give me chastity," he prayed, "give me self-control; but not yet."

The crisis came unexpectedly. He was living in Milan with his friend, Alypius, also a pagan, when one day they were visited by a Christian official on some business matter. During their conversation, he told them about St Anthony and some others who had

The Church of St Sabina in Rome was built early in the 5th century and is a good example of the basilica type. One can see the pillars dividing the building into a nave and two side aisles, the clerestory windows above the pillars, and the semi-circular apse at the far end.

given up everything they had in order to follow Christ; then he took his leave of them. Augustine found himself moved by a strange sadness and went off alone into a quiet corner of the garden.

I threw myself down under a fig tree and gave free rein to my tears, which flowed in torrents, an acceptable sacrifice to you. And I kept saying, if not these words then something very like them: 'How long, O Lord, how long? How long will you be angry, O Lord? For ever? Do not remember the sins of the past.' (I could feel them holding me.) 'How long, how long? Tomorrow and tomorrow? Why not now? Why not this instant put an end to my sinfulness?'

While I was saying this and weeping as if my heart were breaking, I heard a voice from a neighbouring house, the voice of a boy or a girl, I cannot say which, singing over and over again: 'Take and read, take and read.' Immediately my mood changed and I tried to remember if there was any children's game in which these words were sung; but I could not think of any. So I got up and dried my tears, convinced that it was a command from God to open the book and read the first piece I saw. I had heard the story about Anthony happening to come in during the reading of the Gospel and taking the words he heard as if they were addressed especially to himself: 'Go, sell what you possess and give to the poor, and you will have treasure in heaven; and come, follow me;' and by this oracle he was converted to you at once.

So I hurried back to where Alypius was sitting and where I had put down the Book of the Apostle when I left him. I snatched it up, opened it, and read in silence the first piece that met my eyes: 'Not in revelling and drunkenness, not in debauchery and licentiousness, not in quarrelling and jealousy: but put on the Lord Jesus Christ and make no provision for the flesh to gratify its desires.' I read no more: I had no need to. As soon as I had come to the end of that sentence, my heart was flooded with the light of certainty and all the darkness of doubt vanished.

I closed the book, keeping the place by putting in my finger or some other marker, and calmly told Alypius about it. Then he told me what had been going on in his own mind and of which I had known nothing. He asked to see what I had read and I showed it to him. He read on past the place where I had stopped, unaware of what followed. What followed was these words: 'As for the man who is

Right:
The interior of the Church of Sancta Sophia in Constantinople. When the Turks captured the city in 1453 they turned the church into a mosque and made several additions, including the large circular plaques on the walls.

Christ seated in majesty, a 6th century mosaic from the Church of S. Apollinare Nuovo in Ravenna, Italy.

Christ seated in majesty, a full-page illustration from the *Book of Kells*.

weak in faith, welcome him.' These words, he said, applied to himself. And they decided him to join me in my good resolution without any fuss or delay, which was very typical of his character, so much better than my own.

We go in to my mother. We tell her. She is overjoyed. We describe everything that has happened; she is filled with happiness and triumph and blesses you who give us so much more than we ask or think to ask; because she saw that you had granted her more than she had ever desired, among all her sorrowful tears and sighing. You had so completely converted me to yourself that I did not want to marry or gain any worldly ambition; but I took my stand on the rule of faith, as you had shown me doing in that vision you granted her many years before. You turned her sorrow into joy, a greater joy than she had asked for, more pure and precious than the joy of being the grandmother of my children.

Monica died soon afterwards, happy to see her son not only a Christian but resolved to choose the religious life in place of the honourable marriage she had planned for him. He returned to Africa, where he became Bishop of Hippo and began the writings that have made his name immortal. While the cities of the West were falling one by one to the barbarians (Rome was sacked in 410 by the Goths) and the end of civilisation and of Christianity seemed to be near, he refused to despair and began work on his great book *The City of God* to remind men that their true home could not be destroyed by any human enemy. His own city of Hippo was under attack by the Vandals when he died in 430, encouraging and inspiring his people to the end.

The Call of the Desert

The story which contributed to Augustine's conversion was taken from a famous book by St Athanasius, *The Life of St Anthony*. Anthony was one of the first of the Desert Fathers, those men who took the command of Jesus at its most literal and sold or gave away everything they possessed. He went to live in the Egyptian desert, where he passed his time in prayer, work and solitude; despite the austerity of his life, it is said that he was more than a hundred years old when he died in 356.

After the end of the persecution, the call of the desert began to sound in the ears of many of the most committed Christians. They could no longer die for Christ, but they could live for him by putting aside all worldly ambitions, including marriage, and by leading a life of prayer and poverty. They went into the deserts of Egypt and Syria, where they settled in huts and caves and supported themselves by weaving baskets and mats from palm leaves.

As time went by, communities began to form among them. A number of hermits would build their huts near one another, share a common church, and choose one of themselves to be their leader. In this way the first monasteries and convents were formed.

The religious life, as it later came to be called, was a natural growth. No one sat down and invented it. It arose spontaneously from the desire of generous souls to follow Christ as closely as possible. Mistakes were made from time to time in those early days and some people went to extreme lengths to show their contempt for worldly values. There were hermits who walled themselves inside their cells, who went to live on top of high pillars, who even pretended to be insane. It was partly to control the fanatics that each of the first communities drew up a rule of life for itself, laying down poverty, chastity and obedience as the main values to be preserved.

Many stories were told about these first monks and

The octagonal Church of San Vitale in Ravenna, Italy, was built during the reign of Justinian and is in the Byzantine rather than the Roman style.

DOMINVS ECCLESIAE
CONSER PVDENT
VATOR ANAE

nuns and these were gathered together under the
general title of *The Sayings of the Fathers*. This
collection became one of the most popular religious
books of all time. It had a deep and lasting effect on
Christianity in both East and West, and selections
from it are still being bought and read today. The
combination of simplicity and wisdom is very close to
the spirit of the Gospels themselves:

A certain monk named Serapion owned a Book of the Gospels, and he sold it and gave the money to the hungry in accordance with its teaching. And he said: 'I have sold the book that kept saying to me: Sell all you have and give to the poor.'

★

A certain brother had sinned and the priest ordered him out of the church. Bessarion rose up and went out with him saying: 'I too am a sinner.'

★

There was a certain elder who lived in the desert seven miles from the nearest water, and one day when he was going for water he grew weary and said to himself: 'Why should I have to go through all this? I shall move nearer to the water.' Having said this, he turned around and saw someone following him and counting his footprints, and he asked him: 'Who are you?' 'I am an angel of the Lord,' he answered, 'and I have been sent to count your footprints and give you your reward.' When he heard this, the old man's heart was strengthened and he resolved to move still further away from the water.

★

A brother put this question to one of the elders: 'There are two brothers, and one of them stays quietly in his cell, and fasts for six days at a time, and gives himself no comfort; the other looks after the sick. Whose work is the more pleasing to God?' And the elder answered: 'If that brother who fasts for six days at a time were to hang himself up by the nose, he could not equal the other who looks after the sick.'

★

Two elders came once from the region of Pelusium to visit Mother Sara, and on the way they said to one another: 'Let us humble this old woman.' So they said to her: 'Do not give in to pride because men are coming to see you, who are a woman.' And Mother Sara said to them: 'A woman in sex but not in spirit.'

★

The devil appeared to a certain brother as an angel of light and said to him: 'I am the angel Gabriel and I have been sent to you.' But he said: 'Are you sure you were not sent to someone else? I am not worthy to have an angel sent to me.' And the devil disappeared.

★

There were two eiders who lived in the same cell and never had even the slightest disagreement. So one said to the other: 'Let us have just one quarrel like

37

other men do.' And the other said: 'I do not know how to make a quarrel.'

Then the first one said: 'Look, I will put this tile between us and say: This is mine. Then you say: No, it is mine. That is the way to cause a disagreement.'

So they put the tile between them and the first one said: 'That is mine.' The second one answered: 'No, it is mine.'

Then the first one said: 'It is not yours, it is mine.' The second one answered: 'Then take it if it is yours.'

After that they gave up their attempt to start a quarrel.

★

An elder was asked by a soldier if God would receive back a sinner who repented. The elder comforted him saying: 'Tell me, my friend, if your cloak was torn would you throw it away?'

'No,' he answered, 'I would mend it and go on wearing it.'

And the elder said: 'If you would save your cloak, would not God have mercy upon his own image?'

For all their simplicity, the stories and sayings of the Desert Fathers are filled with common sense and religious insight. They are touching accounts of the first attempts to model a way of life entirely on the teachings of Jesus. They still have value and appeal for the reader of today.

Places of Worship

The call of the desert came only to the chosen few: the majority of Christians stayed on in the world. The end of the persecutions solved one problem for them, but it raised others, including the reorganising of the life of the Church to take advantage of the new conditions.

One of the first tasks was to provide fitting places for worship. In all the cities there were elaborate temples built in honour of the gods of paganism; the Christians were determined to do equal honour to their God. Throughout the Roman Empire they began to build churches.

They did not take the pagan temples as models for their church buildings. The temples were magnificent on the outside, with statues and friezes and rows of pillars, but inside they were quite small and few people entered them except the pagan priests.

The Christians, on the other hand, wanted places of worship where there was room for everybody. So they modelled their churches not on the temples but on the basilicas, those large Roman buildings which were used for law courts, public meetings and other such functions. These basilicas were plain on the outside; but inside, because of their large size, they had rows of pillars to support the roof. Often there was a kind of semicircular alcove called an apse in one of the walls; in this the chair of the judge or presiding officer could be set up.

The churches which were begun in Rome during the time of Constantine all followed the basilica pattern. They were long oblong buildings with the main entrance at one end; as the worshipper entered, the first thing he saw was the apse at the far end, containing the altar. On either side were rows of pillars supporting the roof and dividing the church into a central nave and two side aisles. The roof of the nave was one storey higher than the roofs of the aisles and there were windows in this extra storey to make the centre of the church bright; this is called the clearstorey or clerestory.

This simple and practical kind of church was copied widely throughout the Empire, especially in the western part. Even today, many churches still follow the pattern that is now more than sixteen centuries old, with a nave and two side aisles separated by pillars, with the main door at one end and the altar at the

Christ before Pilate, a mosaic from the Church of S. Apollinare Nuovo in Ravenna, period of Justinian.

other. It was not the only pattern used in the West: there were also square churches, round churches and churches in the shape of crosses. But the four great churches built in Rome in the fourth century — St Peter's, St Paul's, St John Lateran, St Mary Major — all followed the basilica pattern with minor variations.

The straightforward Roman style was not so popular among the Greek-speaking Christians of the eastern Empire. They preferred their church buildings to be more subtle and mysterious. They replaced straight lines by curves, clear daylight by a dim radiance, flat ceilings by cunning arrangements of vaults and domes. They developed that style which came to be called Byzantine, after Byzantium, the old name for Constantinople, and which reached its highest peak in the church of Sancta Sophia (Holy Wisdom).

In the year 532 the old church of Sancta Sophia in Constantinople was burnt to the ground. This was early on in the reign of Justinian I, the greatest of the eastern emperors, who ruled from 527 to 565. Justinian was a man of boundless energy and ambition, who made it his life-work to uphold Christian civilisation in a world that was beginning to fall back into barbarism. He sent his great general, Belisarius, from one country to another, to drive back the enemies of the Empire and to recover the lost provinces of Africa and Italy and Spain. He revised the entire body of Roman law and provided a Christian framework for the legal systems of Europe. He involved himself actively in all the affairs of the Church, theology, liturgy, administration, with the best of intentions but not always with the best of results.

The burning of Sancta Sophia gave him another opportunity of making a lasting contribution to the Christian heritage. Some idea of Justinian's hard-driving methods can be gathered from the fact that the new Sancta Sophia was designed and completed in five years, an incredibly short time for what is still regarded as one of the most remarkable buildings in the world.

The Byzantine architects had already solved the problem of building a dome on a square building in small churches; now they succeeded in roofing the new Sancta Sophia with a dome that was 107 feet in diameter. The huge central area of the church was completely without pillars or supports. A cluster of apses, arches, and half-domes acted as spring-boards from which the great central dome soared into space. The interior was decorated sumptuously with rich marbles brought from every part of the Empire and with the work of the finest artists in mosaics. When

Justinian entered the completed building, he gave thanks to God for enabling him to surpass the glory of King Solomon, who built the first temple in Jerusalem.

From the very beginning, people spoke of the prayerful atmosphere of Sancta Sophia. It was not just a building in which God could be worshipped. It was an act of worship in itself. Everything in it helped the worshipper to draw nearer to God. The subdued light filtering from windows around the base of the dome drew the soul gently upwards, away from the things of earth. At night time, with the flickering of countless lamps reflected in the marbles and mosaics until they were lost in the shadows above, the feeling of awe and mystery was even more overwhelming. Sancta Sophia was not a secular-type building adapted to religious use. It was a religious building in which every brick contributed to the glory of God.

The dome of the great church collapsed twenty-one years later as the result of an earthquake. Justinian ordered it to be rebuilt and strengthened. In 563 the eighty-year-old Emperor had the joy of entering the restored church. Two years later he died, but the church he built stands to this day, its beauty hardly dimmed by the passing of the centuries.

Detail of the interior of Sancta Sophia from a nineteenth-century drawing.

Mosaics and Ikons

The artists who decorated the new churches used an exciting new medium, glass mosaics. Designs or pictures made up of hundreds of tiny pieces of different-coloured stone had been in use for several centuries, especially for floors, and these were known as mosaics.

Somewhere around the time of Constantine it was discovered that by using glass instead of stone a much more brilliant and colourful effect could be created. The little cubes of glass were too delicate to be used for flooring but they could be set into walls and ceilings to form decorations and pictures. Rich blues and reds and gleaming whites showed up impressively against a background of glittering gold.

As mosaics became more common, sculpture and painting began to fall into disuse. Few statues of Christ or the saints were made, possibly to avoid any resemblance with the pagan temples which usually contained statues of their gods. Painting still kept some popularity but only because it was cheaper and easier than mosaic; it was looked on as a second-rate substitute for those who could not afford the genuine article.

41

This close-up view of the head of Christ before Pilate shows the small glass cubes from which the mosaic was assembled.

The advantages of mosaic were obvious: its colour, its brilliance, its durability. The main disadvantage was the difficulty of creating any delicate effects of shade or movement when one's material consisted of inch square blocks of stone or glass.

The Byzantine style adapted itself to this difficulty. The figures in a Byzantine mosaic are stiff and formal, their pose is static, their garments fall in straight folds to their feet. To the modern onlooker their faces seem expressionless, with eyes looking straight ahead and no sign of human feeling to be seen. Yet this stillness and remoteness has its own beauty. The Byzantine saints look like people who have moved from time into changeless eternity, serene, dignified, beyond the reach of human passions in a world far different from ours.

The Byzantine artists usually showed Christ and his saints in heavenly glory, not in the pain and sweat of earthly life. Jesus himself was the Pantocrator, that is the Ruler of All Things, a figure of great power and majesty. As time went on, it became customary to place the mosaic of Christ Pantocrator on the curved upper part of the apse over the altar, the most important position in the church. Figures of the Blessed Virgin carrying her child, of angels, of saints, and of important officials of church and state, covered the other walls and ceilings.

The human side of Christ was something that the Byzantine artists neglected; indeed, they seemed to avoid it deliberately. The sufferings and death of Christ were rarely pictured, the cross was shown as a sign of triumph, jewelled and shining and without the figure of Jesus. The crucifixion was something too painful for the Christians of that time to look upon. The memories of persecution were still too fresh.

About the fourth century, the appearance of Jesus began to become standardised in art. During the earlier period he had often been shown as a beardless, short-haired Roman. Now a new image appeared and eventually replaced the older one. It is the image which is familiar to us today, of a man in his thirties, with oval face, regular features, dark shoulder-length hair parted in the middle, moustache and short beard. It seems likely that this image must have been based on memories or descriptions of the appearance of Jesus or even on pictures which are now lost; it is difficult to explain otherwise why such a radical change should have been so widely and quickly accepted. Our present-day image of Jesus cannot be too far away from the historical reality.

A 15th century ikon from Constantinople showing the Virgin and Child, now in the National Gallery of Ireland. It is little different in style from the ikons of a thousand years earlier.

By the time of Justinian's death, religious art was turning into an important industry, especially in the East. Everyone wanted to have an ikon (Greek for image), a painting of Christ or of the Blessed Virgin or of one of the popular saints. These were produced in huge numbers and given the place of honour in homes and work-places, with lights or incense burning in front of them. Though they were generally painted on small wooden panels, they were in the style of the mosaics, with faces and figures posed stiffly against a golden background. They brought a gleam of eternity into people's everyday lives.

The immense popularity of these ikons in the East gave rise to one of the strangest episodes in the history of Christianity, the iconoclast controversy. The respect for ikons became tainted by superstition and many simple people prayed to them as if they were the saints they represented. Others then went to the opposite extreme and said that it was sinful and blasphemous to make images of Christ and the saints and that all such images should be destroyed.

43

The controversy became so heated that the peace of the Empire was in danger. In 726 Emperor Leo III took the side of the iconoclasts or image breakers and he started a campaign to destroy all religious art works in the Empire which lasted under his successors for more than a hundred years. Statues were broken, frescoes painted over, mosaics chipped from walls, pictures hunted out and burnt. The defenders of the ikons often met force with force and many of them were killed or mutilated or imprisoned. It was not until 843 that the power of the iconoclasts was finally broken and the ikons restored to their places.

The whole sad episode dealt a blow to Byzantine art from which it never recovered. Many of the great masterpieces had been destroyed and the development of the artistic traditions had been fatally interrupted. From this time on, Byzantine art became more timid and conservative and anything new was frowned on. Painters turned out copies of copies in a style that hardly changed from one century to the next.

The iconoclast frenzy did not affect the West, where by then the emperors of Constantinople had little authority. Pope Gregory II stated the Catholic position admirably in a few words: "Images are neither to be adored nor destroyed." By a strange irony, the greatest surviving masterpieces of early Byzantine art are in the town of Ravenna in Italy which was recovered from the barbarians by Justinian but lost again after his death.

Among the great mosaics in Ravenna are one of the Emperor Justinian with his courtiers and a matching one of his beautiful wife Theodora with her ladies-in-waiting. They gaze at one another across the church of San Vitale, benign and impassive. They could not have guessed that the Empire patched together by Justinian would fall back again so soon into the hands of the barbarians; or that the same barbarians would preserve and develop the art that Justinian's own successors would destroy.

CHAPTER THREE

THE DARK AGES

On the night of December 31, 406, the Roman sentries
on the river Rhine heard a terrifying sound coming
through the darkness from the far bank, the sound of a
vast army poised for invasion. Soon they could see the
whole surface of the river covered with human forms,
rafts crowded with warriors, men and horses
swimming or clinging to floating tree trunks, barbaric
swords and helmets glittering in the frosty air. Within
minutes the invaders were landing on the Roman side
of the river and the few defenders either ran for their
lives or were massacred where they stood. The days of
the Roman Empire in the West were numbered.

That fateful night was neither the beginning nor the
end of the barbarian invasions, but it was the turning
point. For centuries before that they had been pressing
against the frontiers of the Empire, held back only by
the military power of Rome. For centuries after that
they continued to pour across the Rhine and the
Danube, wave after wave, each savage tribe being
pushed forward by a still more savage one behind it. It
was the most wide-ranging movement of population in
the whole of history and it was to be six centuries
before Europe returned again to stability.

The aim of the barbarians was not to destroy the
Empire but to enjoy its benefits. They envied the
settled and prosperous life of those who lived there and
they wanted to share their good fortune. They pressed
on into France, into Italy, into Spain, into Africa, long
straggling columns of men, women and children,
driving their cattle before them as they marched,
Goths, Vandals, Burgundians, Franks, Lombards, and
many others. The men, tall and fair-haired and blue-
eyed, fought fiercely when they were opposed. When
they were not opposed or when they had defeated their
opponents, they shared out the rich farming lands
among themselves and settled down.

Wherever the barbarians settled, civilisation
crumbled. For the most part they were not deliberately
destructive, they were merely ignorant. They knew so
little about farming that they turned fertile countries
into deserts. Living in towns was beyond them, so the
Roman towns decayed. The Roman aqueducts fell into
ruin, the Roman roads became choked with weeds.
When Alaric the Goth captured the city of Rome itself
in 410, the whole civilised world was horrified; but he

The ruins of a Roman aqueduct in France. Some of these aqueducts were demolished by the barbarians to provide stones for their houses.

himself had no idea what to do with his conquest. For six days he paraded around the city in his great two-horned helmet, while his men robbed and plundered all around them. Then the Goths abandoned the city and set off again on their wanderings in search of food.

The centuries which followed the end of the Roman Empire in the West are known as the Dark Ages. While Europe fell apart into a patchwork of squabbling tribes, there was only one institution which kept the light of civilisation flickering in the darkness. That was the Church.

The civil administration in the West slowly came to a standstill as the legions were drawn back to defend Constantinople and the government officials followed them. The Church administration kept going in spite of all the difficulties. In many places the local bishop was the only symbol of authority remaining, the only link with the old days of law and order. It was often to him that the people turned as crisis followed crisis in those troubled days.

In the city of Rome itself, the Pope became regarded not just as its bishop but as its protector and leader. In 452 the city was threatened by the Huns, the most cruel and merciless of all the barbarian tribes. Pope Leo I went out of the city to plead with their leader, Attila, who had already earned himself the nickname "the scourge of God". The barbarian was so overawed by the brave and saintly old man that he agreed to spare the city in return for a ransom and to go back the way he had come. From then on the Pope was the real ruler of the city of Rome.

Some of the barbarians were pagan, others were Christians of a sort, having been converted to a debased form of the Arian heresy. The work of preaching the Gospel was difficult and dangerous. There were to be many setbacks and many martyrs, but the work went steadily on for century after century until the message of Christianity had been brought to all the peoples of Europe.

The Conversion of the Irish

One of the first of the barbarian peoples to be converted to Christianity was the Irish. The Irish were called barbarians because they had never formed part of the Roman Empire but they were quite different from the other barbarian tribes of the time. They were not uncouth wanderers but a settled people who farmed the land and even had a primitive form of writing. They did not want to leave their own country and invade the Empire, although as the Roman power declined they made occasional pirate raids on the Roman settlements in Britain and brought slaves and treasures back to Ireland.

One of these slaves was a young Christian boy named Patrick, who was to become the apostle of Ireland. At the end of his life Patrick was to write his *Confession*, which was obviously inspired by St Augustine's book and which was a short work thanking God for using him to convert the Irish. It was written in Latin and was, as far as we know, the first book ever written in Ireland.

> I am Patrick, a sinner, the most unlearned of men, the lowliest of all the faithful, utterly worthless in the eyes of many. My father was Calpornius who was a deacon and a son of the priest Potitus. He ministered in a suburb of Bannaven Taberniae where he had a country residence nearby.
>
> It was there that I was taken captive. I was about sixteen years of age at the time and I did not know the true God. I was taken into captivity to Ireland with many thousands of people. We deserved this fate because we had turned away from God; we neither kept his commandments nor obeyed our pastors who used to warn us about our salvation.

Among the pagan Irish, Patrick did not lose his faith. On the contrary, he recovered it. His conversion

47

was less dramatic than Augustine's but it was just as profound.

When I had come to Ireland I tended herds every day and I used to pray many times during the day. More and more my love of God and reverence for him began to increase. My faith grew stronger and my zeal so intense that in the course of a single day I would say as many as a hundred prayers and almost as many in the night. This I did even when I was in the woods and on the mountain. Even in times of snow or frost or rain I would rise before dawn to pray. I never felt the worse for it; nor was I in any way lazy because, as I now realise, I was full of enthusiasm.

In my sleep there one night I heard a voice saying to me: 'It is well that you fast, soon you will go to your own country.' After a short while I again heard a voice saying: 'Look, your ship is ready.' It was quite a distance away, about two hundred miles; I had never been to the place, nor did I know anyone there. I ran away and left the man with whom I had spent six years. The power of God directed my way successfully and nothing daunted me until I reached that ship.

The Gallarus oratory in Co. Kerry is thought to be the oldest church in Ireland. Its exact date is unknown.

Back in Britain with his relatives, Patrick could not forget the Irish. He had another dream one night in which a man named Victoricus seemed to bring him letters from Ireland:

He gave me one and I read the opening words which were: 'The voice of the Irish.' As I read the beginning of the letter I seemed at the same moment to hear the voice of those who were by the wood of Voclut which is near the Western Sea. They shouted with one voice: 'We ask you, boy, come and walk once more among us.' I was cut to the very heart and could read no more, and so I woke up. Thank God, after many years the Lord answered their cry.

Patrick returned as a bishop to the country he had left as a runaway slave. An old tradition puts his return in the year 432, though some scholars think it may have been a little later. During the years that followed he preached throughout the country, baptising converts, ordaining priests, founding churches. As success followed success, he never ceased to wonder at everything that God had accomplished through him:

How then does it happen that in Ireland a people who in their ignorance of God always worshipped idols and unclean things in the past, have now become a people of the Lord and are called children of God? How is it that the sons and daughters of Irish chieftains are seen to be monks and virgins dedicated to Christ?

The *Confession* of St Patrick is not a great work of literature, as he himself was the first to admit: "Anyone can see from the style of my writing how little training in the use of words I got." The book shows the clumsiness one would expect from a man whose education had been so brutally interrupted; but it also shows the humility and courage of a great saint.

Celtic Christianity

The fact that Patrick could speak of the children of chieftains becoming monks and nuns showed how quickly the idea of the religious life took root in Ireland. A style of life which was hard enough in the desert of Egypt took on new hardships when it was transplanted to the cold and rainswept plains of Ireland. Yet these hardships seemed to be a challenge which attracted the most generous-hearted among the new Christians.

During the sixth century monasteries for men and

49

Picture of a lion from the **Book of Durrow**. The artist does not appear to have ever seen a real lion.

women were founded throughout the country. As buildings they were not impressive and normally consisted of a cluster of little huts around a small chapel. But their influence was immense, both at home and abroad. As the Irish had no towns of any size, these monasteries became their principal meeting places. The local bishop usually lived at the monastery and was regarded as less important than the abbot. Each monastic settlement was a centre of learning, a school of holiness, a storehouse of books, a treasury of art. Everything that was sought by the higher nature of man could be found in the monastery.

The most important legacy that these monasteries have left is their manuscripts. In the monastery scriptorium or writing-room, skilled penmen made copies of the Gospels, the Psalms, and other books, including some of the old pagan authors. They wrote on vellum, a kind of fine leather, so that their books would survive centuries of handling; many of these manuscript books are still preserved today.

They had a special reverence for the Gospels, since these contained the words and deeds of the Son of God himself. This reverence made them copy them out with special care and gradually led to a completely new approach to the writing of books. Up to this, a book had been a means of preserving a message and nothing more; what was important was the message in the book, not the book itself. Now the idea began to spread that the actual book should be a thing of beauty, that its artistry should pay homage to the message it contained and help the reader to understand it more fully.

The manuscripts which survive show how this idea developed. One of the earliest is the *Cathach*, a copy of the Psalms said to have been made by St Columcille himself in the sixth century; it is written in a clear and elegant script but a slight embroidering of some capital letters is the only decoration it includes. The *Book of Durrow*, from the seventh century, has much more elaborately decorated capitals, a wider range of colours, and whole pages given over to depicting the symbols of the evangelists, such as a snarling lion for St Mark.

The *Book of Kells*, from the late eighth or early ninth century, carries the art of Celtic decoration to its highest point. It has been called the most beautiful book in the world. The decorated capital letters have now expanded to fill entire pages with an intricate pattern of spirals and interwoven tracery. The interlacing is done with such delicacy and precision that it can barely be followed by the naked eye. All

Right:

The Cross of Muiredach at Monasterboice, Co. Louth. It is almost 18 ft in height and is regarded as one of the finest of the Irish High Crosses.

through the text there are unexpected appearances of birds, animals, men, a face peering through the middle of a letter, a cat scratching herself in the space after a word, two hens finding room for a fight between one line and the next.

In addition to these, there are full-page illustrations of people and incidents from the Gospel story, such as the Virgin and Child, the temptation in the desert, the arrest of Jesus. The scenes are not particularly realistic to a modern eye. The figures are stiff and strained in a manner that recalls the style of the Byzantine ikons. They are meant to move and inspire the reader rather than to impart accurate information about people and events, and in this they succeed perfectly. Almost by accident the copyist has become a painter, the book has become a work of art.

The artistry that went into the making of these books showed itself also in metal and stone. The Irish skill in metalwork was turned to the service of the Church and produced such masterpieces as the Ardagh chalice. The Irish fondness for putting up stone monuments led to the magnificent High Crosses of the ninth and tenth centuries.

The earliest crosses were quite primitive and consisted of the outline of a cross carved on a standing stone or pillar. Then with increasing skill and confidence the carvers began to shape the stones into crosses of a rather unusual kind: the typical Celtic cross had a stone circle where the arms met, possibly in order to prevent them from being broken off.

The decoration of these crosses went through the same kind of development as the decoration of the manuscripts. At first the designs were mostly abstract, with the same intricate interlacing that was used in books and metalwork. Later on animals and men were introduced and the whole surface of the cross was divided into panels, each containing a scene from the Bible or the lives of the saints. These later crosses sometimes displayed fifteen or twenty different picture stories, telling the whole history of salvation from Adam and Eve to Christ on the cross, and from the sending out of the twelve apostles to the Last Judgment.

For those who could not read, the High Crosses took the place of books. Some monasteries had three or four of these great crosses placed around the church to arrest the attention of the passer-by. A thousand years of wind and rain and frost have worn away the carvings and it is no longer possible to make out many of the details. But when they were first erected they were

Bibles in stone, each one an education in itself.

The wise men adoring the child Jesus, a panel from the Cross of Muiredach. Many of the panels are so worn that one can only guess at the subject they represent.

Benedict and Gregory

The rapid conversion of the Irish to Christianity was an unusual event. Elsewhere in Europe, the work of preaching to the barbarians was slower and more difficult. The Irish themselves took part in the work of spreading their new-found faith. Among the early Irish missionaries was St Columcille, the apostle of Scotland, and St Columbanus, who travelled in France, Germany, Switzerland and Italy, and founded several famous monasteries. These monasteries followed the same rule and customs as the ones in Ireland and one custom they introduced into Europe was the practice of private confession. Instead of public penances for public sins, people now began to confess their sins (including their secret sins) to a priest in private and to receive from him a penance which they performed in private.

The Irish monastic rule, on the other hand, was found to be too harsh and most of the continental monasteries, including those founded by Irishmen, changed over eventually to the Benedictine rule. This took its name from Benedict of Nursia, who founded a

53

A portrait of St Benedict by the 15th century Dutch artist, Hans Memling. It captures the gentle serenity of the saint's writings.

monastery at Monte Cassino in Italy in the year 529 and drew up a rule of life for the monks which has formed the basis for monastic life in the West right up to the present day.

The rule of St Benedict is notable for its gentleness and moderation. Though the life it describes is simple and austere, it avoids the extravagant penances that we find in the rules of St Columbanus and others. It lays great emphasis on praying together at fixed times throughout the day, particularly by reciting psalms; this regular prayer is called the Divine Office. The number of psalms to be said is less than in the Irish rules and Benedict makes sure that prayer is balanced by work and sleep; he even allows an afternoon siesta in the hot summer months. He does not merely state rules, he gives the reasoning behind the rules. Chapter 48, dealing with the monk's work, begins in this way:

Idleness is the enemy of the soul. Therefore the brothers should spend certain times at manual work and other times at reading holy books. For this reason, we consider it necessary to make regulations about both of these.

From Easter until the first of October, they should go out at seven o'clock in the morning and work until ten, doing whatever is necessary. From ten to twelve o'clock approximately, they should spend their time reading.

After their midday meal, they should rest on their beds and observe complete silence. If anyone wants to read during this time, he should take care not to disturb the others.

If local conditions or poverty force them to spend the entire day harvesting, they should not be saddened: because they are truly being monks when they are living by the work of their hands, as did our Fathers and the apostles.

Everything is to be done in moderation, however, for the sake of the faint-hearted.

Benedict's kindness and thoughtfulness shine through that last sentence. He knew that monks were human and that they should not be given burdens too heavy to bear. The faint-hearted were to be encouraged, not crushed. For Benedict, God was not a stern taskmaster but a loving father.

The attention given to divine worship was an important element in the Benedictine rule. One of Benedict's greatest admirers was a Roman monk named Gregory, who was only a child when Benedict died but who collected and wrote down everything he could find out about him in the book which he called *Dialogues*. Gregory was elected Bishop of Rome in 590 and soon showed himself to be one of the most outstanding Popes of the Dark Ages, earning for himself the title of Gregory the Great. During the fourteen years of his reign, he worked tirelessly to strengthen the Church and to spread it among the barbarians; it was missionaries sent by him who converted the Angles and Saxons, who had invaded and occupied most of England. The leader of these missionaries, St Augustine (not to be confused with St Augustine of Hippo), became the first bishop of Canterbury and is often called the Apostle of England.

As a monk and a follower of Benedict, Gregory cared deeply about the dignity of divine worship; as a Pope, he was in a position to take effective steps about it. He was not an innovator or a revolutionary. His method, like Benedict's, was to take and use what was best in the traditions handed down to him.

Gregory paid special attention to the ceremonies of

the eucharist and he laid down the procedure to be followed whenever the Pope said Mass in one of the churches in Rome. As the Pope made his way up the church to his throne behind the altar, the choir sang an entrance song, followed by the *Kyrie. Eleison* (Lord, have mercy) and on certain days the *Gloria in excelsis Deo* (Glory to God in the highest). Then the Pope recited a prayer suitable for the particular day. This was followed by two readings from the Bible, the second one always from one of the Gospels; between the two readings a responsory was sung.

After the Gospel, the people came up and presented their gifts of bread and wine to the Pope; these were placed on the altar, which was in the shape of a simple table. The Pope stood behind this, facing the people, and began to say aloud the Eucharistic Prayer. The *Sanctus* (Holy, holy, holy) was sung by the choir. The Pope continued with the Eucharistic Prayer, which was identical with the First Eucharistic Prayer in our present-day Mass. However, the action of holding up the bread and the chalice after the words of consecration had not come in.

Before the communion, the *Pater Noster* (Our Father) was sung by the Pope and all present exchanged the kiss of peace with those next to them. While the assistant bishops and priests were dividing up the consecrated bread for Holy Communion, the choir sang the *Agnus Dei* (Lamb of God). The people received it in their hands and when they had eaten it were given the chalices to drink from. At the same time, the choir was singing a communion psalm.

After the communion, the Pope said the post-communion prayer. Then a deacon sang *Ite, missa est* (Go, the Mass is ended) and the answer was given *Deo gratias* (Thanks be to God). The Pope then left the church and the ceremony was over.

The resemblance between the Mass as said by St Gregory and the Mass of today is clear, and the changes brought about by the Second Vatican Council have made that resemblance even clearer. The important part played by the choir is also clear. Gregory went to great trouble to have suitable chants for the different parts of Mass and of the Divine Office and to have them sung by trained choirs. Under his guidance, music became another way of adorning the worship of God, along with art and architecture and solemn ceremonial. The music was plain chant or plain song, sung without harmonies (which is why it was called plain) and it had to be learnt by heart, as no way of writing down music had yet been discovered. But in

Left:
The Emperor Charlemagne on horseback, a small bronze statue which probably dates from the time of Charlemagne himself.

spite of its plainness, it had great dignity and expressiveness. Later writers often called it Gregorian chant, because of the part played by Gregory in developing it.

There was one thing which was in danger of being lost in this splendid ceremony and that was the participation of the people. With the singing given over to the choir, the part taken by the congregation was reduced. The process was beginning by which the congregation would be turned into silent spectators.

The Emperor Charlemagne

Still the barbarians came. The Eastern Empire, which had fought off the tribes from the north, suddenly found itself under attack from the south. Fired by the teachings of the prophet Mohammed, who died in 632, the primitive nomads of Arabia launched a Holy War to convert the rest of the world. During the next hundred years the Arabs seized the Holy Land, the whole of North Africa, and most of Spain; Christianity disappeared from all these places. From now on, the Byzantine Empire was an Empire in name only. Greece, Asia Minor, a part of Italy and a few islands were all that remained under its authority.

The decline of the old empire in the East was accompanied by the rise of a new one in the West. In 768 the king of the Franks died and was succeeded by his son, Charles. The Franks were a barbarian tribe who occupied and gave its name to France; they had been converted to Christianity around the year 500. Charles reigned until 814, one of the longest and most glorious reigns in the history of Europe, all the more remarkable by contrast with the chaos which went before it and came after it. In the years after his death he was to become the hero of countless stories, a legendary and almost mythical figure in the folklore of the Middle Ages, known to succeeding generations as Charles the Great or Charlemagne.

All through his reign Charlemagne was engaged in warfare. He saw these wars not as an act of aggression but as a work of civilisation. Compared to some of the other barbarians, the Franks were almost civilised; and in his battles against the Saxons and the Frisians, Charlemagne saw himself as a Christian missionary rather than a conquering soldier. In Spain he curbed the power of the Arabs and prevented them from crossing the mountains into France. In Italy he rescued the Popes from the threat of the Lombards. By the year 800 he was in control of a vast area of Europe, including France, West Germany, the Low Countries

Right:
The round tower at Glendalough, Co. Wicklow. The door is well above ground level for greater protection against Viking raiders.

58

and most of Italy.

On Christmas Day of the year 800, Charlemagne attended Mass in St Peter's Basilica in Rome. As he knelt in prayer, the Pope approached him, placed a crown on his head, and greeted him with the title "Emperor of the Romans". Charlemagne said afterwards that he was taken by surprise and that he would never have entered the church if he had known what was going to happen; but nobody believed him or wanted to believe him. Instead they rejoiced that order and unity had come again to the West and that they had a Christian Emperor once more ruling over them.

It did indeed seem for a time as though civilisation had returned to Europe. The new Emperor's capital city of Aachen in the Rhineland became a centre of culture and learning. Scholars came from England and Ireland, France and Italy, to study and teach in its schools. The writings of older authors were gathered and preserved and copied out with loving care. Manuscripts were illustrated with delicate paintings and enclosed in covers of carved ivory.

The Palace Chapel at Aachen was one of the city's chief glories and is the only one that still survives. It was a massive eight-sided building with three storeys of arches inside supporting a vaulted roof. The West had seen nothing like it since Justinian built San Vitale in Ravenna; indeed, it was said that Charlemagne intended his chapel to rival Justinian's. The labour involved in the building was immense by the standards of the time, but the Emperor's determination overcame all obstacles. The completed chapel proved that the art of architecture had not died for ever and that the barbarians might one day hope to rival and even surpass the builders of ancient Rome.

Within the chapel, the worship of God was conducted with piety and devotion. Charlemagne sent to Rome for the Mass-book of St Gregory and had choirs trained in the singing of Gregorian chant. From the Palace Chapel, the Gregorian form of worship spread throughout the Western Empire and replaced the various local forms. The Emperor himself loved nothing better than to attend Mass or the Divine Office in the chapel he had built.

At the same time, this noble monarch was still half a barbarian. This devout churchgoer had five wives and uncounted mistresses. This Christian missionary converted the Saxons by forcing them to choose between baptism and death. This patron of learning was unable to read or write with any ease. He kept a notebook under his pillow at night so that he could practise writing the alphabet whenever he could not sleep. But with all his contradictions, he remained a hero in the imagination of the people of Europe, courageous, just and generous, the very ideal of the Christian ruler.

According to one story, he had a bell set up outside his palace which anyone seeking justice could ring. One day an old stray horse looking for something to eat nibbled at the bell-rope and rang the bell. The Emperor had it fed and housed in his own stables and punished the callous owner who had turned it loose when it was no longer able to work. The story may be no more than a legend but it says something about Charlemagne that such stories should cling to his name.

There was need of his gracious memory to keep hope alive in the next two centuries. There were still more barbarians to come, and the civilisation established by Charlemagne did not long survive his death. From the East the Hungarians brought fresh terror and destruction, destroying whole cities and killing every living soul within them. From the North the Vikings sailed in search of plunder and even reached Ireland, the only part of Europe that had escaped the previous invaders; the Irish monasteries built their tall round towers as places of refuge from the Norsemen. Saracen pirates from Spain and North Africa raided and robbed the coastlands of the Mediterranean. The Papacy itself fell victim to the intrigues of the barbarians and some of those elected Pope were utterly unworthy of their office. But through the horrors of the ninth and tenth centuries, the ideal of Christian civilisation planted by the great Emperor remained alive. Like a seed hidden in the earth, it only needed favourable conditions to grow and flower and bear fruit.

CHAPTER FOUR

THE MIDDLE AGES

Many people expected the world to come to an end in the year 1000. This belief was based on the mysterious Chapter 20 of the Book of Revelation, which spoke of a thousand-year reign by Christ and his saints and also of a dragon which was to be released on the world after an imprisonment of a thousand years. The belief would not have been as widespread as it was had not the state of the world been so wretched. Things were so bad that they could scarcely be worse. Europe was in a mood of despair.

The year 1000 came and went and the world did not come to an end. Hope began to revive again, encouraged by signs of a turn in the tide. The savage Hungarians received their first Christian king in 1001, the Norwegians in 1016, the Poles in 1025. The ruler of Kiev, Prince Vladimir, established Christianity in Russia before his death in 1015. The Church was no longer on the defensive but was moving out beyond the boundaries of the old Roman Empire

Europe was now becoming a Christian continent. The period which is generally known as the Middle

St John's Chapel in the Tower of London shows the round arches and heavy walls of the Romanesque style.

Ages was beginning, the period of roughly 1000-1500 during which the Church dominated every aspect of European life: art, architecture, literature, music, education, even recreation. It was the age of faith, which was to reach its high point during the thirteenth century and then gradually decline again until it was blown apart by the Reformation at the beginning of the sixteenth century.

At the head of the Church was the Pope, the Bishop of Rome. Below him were the other bishops, one in each important town; the church where the bishop had his throne or *cathedra* was called a cathedral church. The territory in the bishop's charge was a diocese and it was divided up into parishes which corresponded to the country villages, each with its own parish church and parish priest. Independent of the bishop were the Benedictine monasteries or abbeys, with their own churches and lands. A branch of the Benedictines, called the Cistercians, began in 1098 and spread rapidly across the continent, from Ireland to Poland. The number of convents of nuns also began to increase. Europe could now justly call itself Christendom, the realm of Christians.

The Gothic Cathedral

Of all the contributions made by the Middle Ages to the Christian heritage, the most remarkable is the great cathedrals. Many of them still stand today, for they were built to last; and though the builders of the twentieth century can build higher and faster, they cannot build more beautifully.

During the eleventh and twelfth centuries, the cathedrals were built in the style called Romanesque, from its resemblance to the buildings of ancient Rome. This style is marked by the use of round arches; there were semicircular arches over doors and windows, between the pillars of the nave, and as decorations on the outside walls. The roofs were also rounded like the roof of a tunnel, and since they were made of stone they were very heavy and needed massive walls to support them. The Romanesque churches have great solidity and dignity but they have a certain heaviness as well that comes from their thick walls and pillars and small windows.

Towards the end of the twelfth century that heaviness began to vanish as builders and architects became more skilful. A new style of architecture, the Gothic style, appeared in France and spread to other parts of Europe. Its most obvious difference was that round arches were replaced by pointed arches, but

63

Cormac's Chapel on the Rock of Cashel was built between 1127 and 1134 in the Irish Romanesque style. The building in the background is of a later date.

there was more to it than a mere change of shape. There was a whole new approach to the science of building.

What the Gothic architects had done was this: they had discovered the way to construct a framework. The Gothic church was supported by its pillars, not its walls. The arched ribs of the roof were made high and pointed so that they bore down almost vertically upon the pillars of the nave and aisles. These pillars were strengthened outside by heavy pinnacles and by flying buttresses. The space between the pillars could then be closed up as walls or left as windows or open arches.

The interior of St Patrick's Cathedral, Dublin, dating mainly from the 13th century.

St Francis preaching to the birds, a fresco attributed to Giotto in the Basilica at Assisi, Italy.

Head of St Peter,
Chartres Cathedral.

Overleaf:
Amiens Cathedral, France.
Characteristic of French Gothic
are the richly decorated west front,
with statues, porches and rose
window, and the lofty nave
supported by flying buttresses
and pinnacles. The towers, as
often happened, were completed
later than the rest of the building
and do not follow the original
plan.

Right:
The nave of Lincoln Cathedral,
England. The main altar was at
the far end of the building and
could only be glimpsed by the
congregation through the small
doorway under the organ.

This gave great freedom to the architect, who had no longer to make his walls as thick as possible and his windows as small as possible. Once the framework was correctly constructed, he could do as he liked with the rest.

All during the thirteenth century, cathedrals grew higher and wider and more adventurous. Each town tried to outdo its neighbour in magnificence. Sometimes they tried too hard: the cathedral at Beauvais, with the highest roof in France, collapsed twice and was never properly completed. The labour involved was immense, the populations were small, the financial resources were meagre, the building techniques were primitive. Whole forests were cut down to make the wooden scaffolding that enveloped and supported the structure until it was completed. The work could take from fifty to a hundred years, and even then there were usually towers still to be completed or spires to be added. Those who began the work had no hope of living to see it finished but this did not deter them. They were not building for themselves, but for the generations to come, for the faith, for the Church, for the glory of God.

The typical Gothic cathedral followed the Roman basilica plan of a nave and two side aisles. To that it added two transepts, one on each side like the arms of a cross. It was always built so that the altar was at the east end and the main entrance at the west end; the transepts were therefore on the north and south sides. The place where the transepts met the nave was called the crossing and sometimes a tower or spire was built over this. The west front usually had two towers to show its importance, one on each side of the main doorway. In addition, on the outside one could see a wealth of pinnacles and buttresses, not just as decorations but as part of the balance of forces that kept the building upright.

The cathedral offered plenty of opportunities to the sculptor. Angels perched on top of pinnacles, grotesque gargoyles spat out rain water from their gaping mouths. Statues of Christ and the saints stood guard at all the doorways. Scenes from the Bible were carved in the porches to instruct the people as they passed in and out. These sculptures, however, always took second place to the architecture. They did not stand by themselves but were fastened to walls or enclosed in niches. Sculpture was still conceived in relation to its setting, not as an art in itself.

The Gothic cathedral had little in the way of paintings or mosaics but it did have stained glass. The

Detail from **Joan of Arc** by Ingres.

new method of building made it possible to have large windows in all kinds of interesting shapes, including circular or rose-windows. The art of stained glass, which had hardly existed before, took on a sudden importance. Master craftsmen travelled around from one cathedral building site to another, each with his own secret techniques for colouring and cutting glass and forming patterns and pictures that glowed like jewels in the dimness. Like the sculptures, these windows told stories from the Old and New Testaments and the lives of the saints, and at the same time bathed the inside of the church in a soft light of many colours. The secret of this glass was never written down and is now lost. No modern stained glass maker can achieve the same richness and brilliance as the craftsmen of the Middle Ages.

The first great Gothic cathedrals were built in the north of France, most notably in the towns of Paris, Chartres, Rheims and Amiens; there are examples in many other parts of France and of central and northern Europe. Nearly every English town built a Gothic cathedral. Dublin went one better and built two. In addition, there were countless monastery and parish churches built on the same lines, if on a smaller scale. It was a truly international style.

If one stands today in one of these mediaeval churches, one can see why it had so wide an appeal. Everything in the church points heavenwards. The eye is carried up along the clusters of columns, past the sculptured capitals, past the glowing windows, until it is lost in the mysterious intertwining of the vaults high overhead. The outside conveys the same message, a perfect reflection and confirmation of what lies within. In no other style of architecture is there the same unity between interior and exterior, the same matching of means to ends, the same singleness of purpose. Everything in the Gothic cathedral seems to be in movement, a movement towards God.

Religion of the People

The cathedral was the centre of worship in the mediaeval diocese, where Mass was celebrated and the Divine Office said with particular solemnity. There was great devotion to the Mass among the people, whether in the cathedral or in their own parish church, but this devotion was sometimes tinged with superstition and the gulf between the altar and the congregation was growing wider.

The Mass was still said in Latin, though that language was no longer spoken by the people. The altar

was placed against a wall or screen, with the result that the priest had to stand with his back to the congregation. The attitude of prayer for the people was no longer the old Roman one of standing with upraised arms; now they followed the German tradition by kneeling and joining their hands. When they received Holy Communion, which they did very rarely, they received it under the form of bread only and on the tongue, not in the hand. The Blessed

St Peter and another apostle, two statues from the south porch of Chartres Cathedral, France.

69

Stained glass windows in Chartres Cathedral. The photograph shows how the weight of the building is borne by the pillars and roof ribs, so that most of the wall-space can be turned into windows.

Sacrament was regarded with such reverence that people were almost afraid to receive it.

To satisfy this reverence, the custom came in of the priest holding up the host after the consecration so that the people could look at it. This elevation of the host became the high-point of the Mass for the people, and some of them would rush from altar to altar and even from church to church collecting as many elevations as possible. There is a well-known description of a congregation in an English church shouting to the priest as he held up the host: "Hold up, Sir John, hold up. Heave it a little higher." It all added up to a one-sided view of the Mass as something that God gives to man but not as something that man gives to God.

The people were also largely excluded from the music of the Mass, which continued to be based on the

Gregorian chant, though singing in harmony was beginning to come in. The development of musical notation in the eleventh and twelfth centuries made it possible to combine two different melodies. The cathedral of Notre Dame in Paris led the way and its choirmasters Léonin and Pérotin were the first important composers in the history of music. Léonin wrote only two-part music (that is, music that combines two lines of melody together) but Pérotin around 1200 succeeded in writing three- and even four-part music for the cathedral choir. This kind of music became known as polyphony (Greek for many voices) and was used increasingly as composers and choirs became more skilful. The congregation could not join in with this kind of singing, though they could listen to it and be moved to prayer by its beauty.

Something which had a much wider appeal to the people was the Mystery Play. The cathedral clergy used sometimes to dramatise incidents from the Bible to make them more vivid. A monk dressed in white would say the words of the angel at Easter, or three monks wearing crowns would come up the church on the feast of the Epiphany as if they were the wise men coming to Bethlehem. These scenes became so popular that they had to be made longer and more elaborate until they developed into real plays, the first plays that had been seen in Europe since the fall of Rome. They were moved out of the church and performed in the streets of the town, usually on the feast of Corpus Christi, and they covered the whole story of God's dealings with men, from the Creation to the Last Judgment.

The text of some of these Mystery Plays has come down to us and they are occasionally performed today. They mingle theological discourses with dramatic incidents, high tragedy with knockabout farce. Audiences loved scenes where Noah's wife got drunk and refused to go into the ark, or where one of the Bethlehem shepherds tried to steal a sheep by disguising it as a baby. The Massacre of the Innocents gave opportunities for acting to the tyrannous Herod and to the sorrowing mothers. A fifteenth-century English play gives these lines to one of the bereaved women, as she berates the soldier who killed her baby:

Out! Murder-man, I say, strong traitor and thief!
Out, alas, and wellaway! My child that was me lief!
My love, my blood, my play, that never did man grief!
Alas, alas, this day! I would my heart should cleave

Dante Alighieri, detail from the fresco by Domenico di Francesco.

Mediaeval musicians as depicted by a 12th century manuscript. In the centre is an early type of organ, with two men playing it and four men blowing the bellows.

Asunder!
Vengeance I cry and call
On Herod and his knights all.
Vengeance, Lord, on them fall
And mickle world's wonder!

There is poetry here and passion, and it was from plays like these that Shakespeare learned his craft. Indeed, he may have had performances of this very play in mind when he has Hamlet complain about actors who overplay their parts: "I would have such a fellow whipped for overdoing Termagant; it out-herods Herod; I pray you avoid it." There is a direct line of descent between the amateur theatricals of the Mystery Plays and the masterpieces of Shakespeare and his contemporaries.

The coming of the Friars

The Gothic spirit flourished north of the Alps. It never really took root in Italy. The very name "Gothic" was invented by the Italians as an insult: they felt there was something barbarous about it, reminding them of the Goths who plundered Rome in 410. Italy had its own contribution to make to the world of the Middle Ages and it can be summed up by looking at the lives of four remarkable Italians: Francis of Assisi, Thomas Aquinas, Dante Alighieri, and Giotto di Bordone.

Francis was born at Assisi about 1182, the son of a wealthy cloth merchant. He led the life of a young man-about-town until he was about twenty-one; then, after an illness, he suddenly changed and began to devote himself to prayer and almsgiving. He gave away

some cloth belonging to his father who objected strongly and hauled the young man before the local bishop. There followed the famous incident when Francis gave back to his father not only his money and goods but the very clothes off his back. From now on he was resolved to own nothing. He dressed in the coarsest cloth and left his father's house to live in perfect poverty.

An artists's impression of an English mystery play, showing Christ being accused by the high priests before Pilate. The stage was often mounted on a wheeled wagon so that performances could be given in different parts of the town.

73

Francis had no intention of founding any kind of organisation. But others asked if they could join him and he could not turn them away. When he died in 1226 he had hundreds of followers in many countries, all committed to poverty and to the preaching of the word of God. The Franciscans had been born.

They did not call themselves monks but friars, which means brothers. They did not live apart from the world in remote monasteries but in small houses in the towns where they could be in direct contact with the people. Not only their preaching but their whole way of life reminded people of the teaching of the Gospel, that the follower of Christ must give up all his

St Francis in Ecstasy, a painting by El Greco in the National Gallery of Ireland. El Greco's idea of the saint is more spiritual and less human than Giotto's.

worldly goods and take the cross upon his shoulders.

The teaching of Francis might sound gloomy but it was not. By renouncing riches he freed himself to enjoy all the beauties of creation. In his *Song of the Sun* he thanked God for the benefits that others took for granted:

Praise to you, my Lord, for all your creatures,
Above all for Brother Sun
Who brings us day and gives us his light;
He is beautiful and shines with great splendour,
And he tells us of you, most High.

Praise to you, my Lord, for Sister Moon and the stars,
You have set them in the heavens, clear and precious and fair.

Portrait of the Blessed Virgin from Fra Angelico's **Annunciation**.

Praise to you, my Lord, for Brother Wind,
For air and cloud, for calm and all weather,
By which you give nourishment to your creatures.

Praise to you, my Lord, for Sister Water,
Who is so useful and humble, precious and pure.

Praise to you, my Lord, for Brother Fire,
By whom you illumine the night;
He is lovely and joyful, mighty and strong.

Praise to you, my Lord, for our sister Mother Earth,
Who sustains us and directs us
And brings forth different fruit and coloured flowers and grass.

Many stories were told about him after his death and a collection of these was made called *The Little Flowers of Saint Francis*. These are like the stories of the Desert Fathers in their charm and simplicity, though they lack their brevity. How many of them are true it is hard to say, but they certainly preserve the spirit of Francis. One of them tells how he tamed a savage wolf at Gubbio; another has him preaching to a field full of birds:

'My little sisters the birds, you have received many things from God your Maker, and you should praise him everywhere, for he has clothed you with double and triple plumage and given you freedom to fly wherever you will. He has preserved your species in the ark of Noah, so that it should not perish out of the world. Again, you owe to him the element of the air, which he has assigned to you.

75

'Furthermore, you do not sow or reap, yet God feeds you and gives you the rivers and springs to drink from, the mountains and hills for your refuge, and the high trees in which to build your nests. And although you do not know how to spin or sew, God clothes both you and your young. Your Creator shows great love for you, since he has given you so many blessings. So, my little sisters, keep yourselves from the sin of ingratitude, and always strive to praise God.'

As Saint Francis was speaking to them, all the birds began to open their beaks, stretch out their necks, and reverently bow their heads to the ground, showing by their actions and songs that the words of the holy father gave them the greatest delight. And Saint Francis was glad and rejoiced with them, filled with wonder at so great a host of birds, their beauty and variety, their attention to him, and their tameness. And he devoutly praised the Creator in them for all these things.

True or not, stories like these capture the spirit of St Francis. He had never heard of such words as conservation or ecology; but his reverence for God flowed over into a reverence for the world and all that it contained.

Apart from the followers of Francis, there were other groups of friars who came together during the thirteenth century. Among them were the Augustinians, the Carmelites and the Dominicans. The Dominicans took their name from their founder, St Dominic, though they preferred to be known as the Order of Preachers, since they specialised in preaching and writing about the truths of the faith.

This was the time when the first universities were being founded in Europe. Like so many other things, they sprang from the cathedrals. In addition to parish schools, every diocese was supposed to have a cathedral school where a more advanced education could be given to the brighter pupils. Some of these cathedral schools became large and important and in time gained their independence from the local bishop. These were the first universities.

The friars naturally availed of these universities as places in which to study and teach theology. The most famous teacher among the friars was a young Italian nobleman, Thomas Aquinas. When the young man tried to join the Dominicans, his family locked him up for a year, but they could not make him change his mind. He was released, became a Dominican, and spent the rest of his life writing and teaching in such great centres of learning as Paris, Cologne and Naples.

Thomas was large and placid; his schoolmates nicknamed him The Dumb Ox. But he had a mind of tremendous depth and insight and an astounding capacity for work. The number of books written by him is staggering. It is said that he sometimes dictated three or four books at the same time, while the pens of his secretaries raced across the paper in an attempt to keep pace with his thoughts. He was interested in every kind of knowledge, philosophy, theology, psychology, ethics, physics, law. He wrote exquisite Latin poems in honour of the Blessed Sacrament. He was a man of deep spirituality. Shortly before his death in 1274, he said that all his writings seemed like straw compared with what had been revealed to him in his hours of prayer.

The great achievement of St Thomas Aquinas is the way he dealt with the dispute between reason and faith. At that time, the new universities were excitedly discovering the works of the great philosophers of the past. In particular, they were reading Aristotle, the great Greek thinker who lived four centuries before Christ. Many churchmen wanted to have Aristotle's books banned from the universities since they felt they could lead the students astray. Christians had the light of the Gospels for their guide: what could a pagan have to teach them?

St Thomas did not accept this point of view. He held that men who had never heard about Christ could still come to belief in God by looking at the world around them. By using their reasoning powers they could see that the world must have been created by someone, and that this someone must be good and all-powerful and eternal. They could see that their only true happiness lay in coming to know their creator perfectly and they could work out which actions would bring them closer to him and which actions would not. There was no conflict between reason and religion: if a thing was true in philosophy, it was also true in theology. Truth could not be divided against itself.

St Thomas used the teaching of Aristotle as a firm foundation on which to build his philosophy and theology. He had many opponents during his lifetime and afterwards, and the Bishop of Paris condemned some of his opinions in 1277, but such condemnations had no lasting effect. The teaching of Thomas Aquinas, often simply called Thomism, was so clear, so logical, and so wide-ranging, that it was difficult to argue against. His greatest book, the *Summa Theologica* (Summary of Theology) remains today as impressive and as satisfying as the cathedrals which were its contemporaries.

Dante and Giotto

There were many other notable thinkers who came from the mediaeval schools and were known therefore as schoolmen or scholastics. The scholastic philosophers wrote in Latin, whether they came from England or Ireland or France or Germany or Italy; Latin was the international language used for all serious writing. The different languages spoken by the common people of Europe were considered to be unsuitable for literature until the great Italian poet, Dante Alighieri, proved the contrary.

Dante was born in Florence in 1265 and lived there until 1302, when he was forced to leave his beloved city by political enemies. He wandered restlessly around Italy for what remained of his life and died at Ravenna in 1321. Those last nineteen years of his life were bitter for the poet but sweet for the rest of mankind, since it was during those years that he wrote *The Divine Comedy*, the first great work of literature in a modern European language.

VI COELVM CECINIT MEDIVMQVE IMVMQVE TRIBVNAL ✦ LVSTRAVITQVE ANIMO CVNCTA POETA SVO ✦ DOCTVS ADEST DANTES SVA QVEM FLORENTIA SAEPE ✦ ENSIT CONSILIS AC PIETATE PATREM ✦ NIL POTVIT TANTO MORS SAEVA NOCERE POETAE ✦ QVEM VIVVM VIRTVS CARMEN IMAGO FACIT ✦

Dante's reason for writing in Italian was not that he was ignorant of Latin. On the contrary, he had read all the classics of ancient Rome and he knew the *Aeneid*, the epic poem by Virgil, almost by heart. He was also a keen admirer of Thomas Aquinas and was thoroughly familiar with his writings. The combination of the pagan poet and the Christian philosopher were to result in a magnificent epic poem which spanned the height of Heaven and the depth of Hell, and touched every human emotion in between.

The Divine Comedy is not a comedy in the modern sense of the word. It is an account in beautiful rhymed verse of an imaginary journey by the poet through the regions of the dead, which is supposed to have happened between Good Friday and Easter Sunday of the year 1300; the inspiration for it comes from the sixth book of Virgil's *Aeneid*, which describes the visit of Aeneas to the underworld. Dante divides his poem into three sections, corresponding to the three stages of his journey; they are called *Inferno, Purgatorio* and *Paradiso* — Hell, Purgatory and Heaven.

The poem begins with Dante lost in a dark wood and threatened by wild animals. He is rescued by a man who turns out to be none other than the poet Virgil, who is to be his guide through the underworld. He

Dante and his Poem, a painting by Domenico di Francesco in Florence Cathedral. Hell is on the left and Purgatory in the centre. The idealised picture of Florence on the right may be meant to represent heaven.

79

leads Dante through a gate over which are written the words: "All hope abandon, ye who enter here." It is the gate of Hell:

> Here sighs with lamentations and loud moans
> Resounded through the air pierced by no star,
> That e'en I wept at entering. Various tongues,
> Horrible languages, outcries of woe,
> Accents of anger, voices deep and hoarse,
> With hands together smote that swelled the sounds,
> Made up a tumult that for ever whirls
> Round through that air with solid darkness stained,
> Like to the sound that in the whirlwind flies.

They descend through the nine circles of Hell, where sinners suffer the punishment of their sins. Dante asks many of them for the stories of their lives, and the stories of the guilty love of Paolo and Francesca or of the last voyage of Ulysses or of the death of Count Ugolini and his family, are among the most touching parts of the poem. Finally they pass through the lowest circle, where Lucifer is encased in ice, and find themselves at the foot of the mountain of Purgatory.

Dante and Virgil make the weary climb up the seven terraces of Purgatory and on each they find sinners being cleansed of one of the deadly sins. The atmosphere here is very different from the despair of Hell. It is a place of suffering but also a place of hope:

> As the blind man behind his leader walks,
> Lest he should err or stumble unawares
> On what might harm him or perhaps destroy,
> I journeyed through that bitter air and foul,
> Still listening to my escort's warning voice,
> 'Look that from me thou part not.' Straight I heard
> Voices, and each one seemed to pray for peace
> And for compassion to the Lamb of God
> That taketh sins away. Their prelude still
> Was 'Agnus Dei', and through all the choir
> One voice, one measure ran, that perfect seemed
> The concord of their song. 'Are these I hear
> Spirits, O master?' I exclaimed; and he,
> 'Thou aim'st aright: these loose the bonds of wrath.'

The summit of the mountain is the threshold of Heaven. Virgil, the pagan, can go no further and from here on Dante is guided by Beatrice, a girl whom he had loved in boyhood and who died young. Together they rise effortlessly through the nine spheres of

Heaven, meeting and speaking to many saints on the way. Dante is overjoyed to meet Thomas Aquinas, who introduces him to other great philosophers and describes the true nature of wisdom. They come at last to the ninth Heaven, the end of their journey:

Then 'Glory to the Father, to the Son,
And to the Holy Spirit,' rang aloud
Throughout all Paradise; that with the song
My spirit reeled, so passing sweet the strain.
And what I saw was equal ecstasy:
One universal smile it seemed of all things;
Joy past compare; gladness unutterable;
Imperishable life of peace and love;
Exhaustless riches, and unmeasured bliss.

In the ninth sphere, Dante sees the greatest saints and the Blessed Virgin and finally is allowed to look upon the majesty of God, to describe which is to describe the indescribable. The poem ends here; the poet can say no more.

This vast epic is one of the undisputed masterpieces of world literature. It is not always easy to understand; many of the details have allegorical meanings and are not meant to be taken literally. It is possible also to find fault with some of the theological views, such as the excluding from Heaven of Virgil and other good pagans. But these defects are slight compared with the sublimity of Dante's vision and the beauty of the language in which he describes it, a beauty that survives even in an English translation.

Among those mentioned favourably by Dante in his poem is the painter Giotto di Bordone. Giotto was born in Florence a year or two after Dante and died in 1337. The two men were friends but it was not friendship alone that caused Dante to praise him; for Giotto was almost as great a genius as Dante himself.

The churches of Italy kept to the old Romanesque style rather than the newer Gothic, since thick walls and small windows were an advantage rather than a disadvantage in that hot climate. This style of building gave little scope for stained-glass work but it provided a fine opportunity for the painter: the large wall-spaces were ideal for pictures. A method was discovered of painting directly on to fresh plaster; such paintings were called frescoes (*fresco* is the Italian for "fresh") and became a very popular form of decoration in Italian churches and houses.

Giotto's first important assignment was to paint frescoes on the walls of the new church built at Assisi

The Annunciation, by Fra
Angelico. Its innocence and tenderness make it one of the best loved
of all religious pictures.

in honour of St Francis. These frescoes, showing
scenes from the life of the saint, were the first clear-cut
break with the old Byzantine style. Instead of stiff
supernatural figures gazing out impassively from a
golden background, Giotto painted human beings who
had weight and shape, who looked at one another
rather than out at the spectator, who existed in a world
of recognisable houses and mountains and trees. His
treatment of a scene like Francis preaching to the birds
is charming in its freshness and simplicity. Each bird is
an individual portrait with its own plumage and its
own attitude, and the whole picture shows a feeling for
nature that Francis would surely have enjoyed. The
same naturalness and freshness is to be found in the
scenes from the Gospels that Giotto painted in a
church at Padua, the same feeling that a new style of
painting had been born. It is with good reason that he
has been called the Father of Modern Painting.

Giotto chose religious themes for all his paintings
and the same can be said of most of his followers. The
fourteenth and fifteenth centuries saw a long line of
gifted painters in Florence and other Italian cities who
made Italy the leader and teacher of Europe in the art
of painting. It would be impossible even to list their
names here, but mention must be made of one painter
who was regarded even in his own lifetime as

outstanding for the sincerity of his religious paintings. He was Fra Angelico.

Fra Angelico was a Dominican friar who spent most of his life in Florence and painted many frescoes on the walls of the friary there as an aid to prayer and meditation. He died in Rome in 1455. He was by all accounts a man of great holiness and humility, who never took up his brush without first saying a prayer for guidance and who was often seen to weep as he painted scenes of the passion and crucifixion. His pictures have an other-worldly quality which combines the naturalism of Giotto with the serenity of the Byzantine artists. In itself, piety is not enough to make a good religious painting; but when it is combined with technical mastery, as it was in the case of Fra Angelico, it produces something quite special. Fra Angelico was perhaps the only great artist who was also a saint, and it shows in all his work.

The decline of the Middle Ages

The fifteenth century marked the end of the Middle Ages. It was not a happy century and it showed ominous signs of the yet greater troubles that were to come. The biggest blow, and one which horrified all Europe, was when the Turks captured the city of Constantinople in 1453 and put an end to what remained of the old Roman Empire in the East. The last of the Eastern emperors was killed during the assault and the church of Sancta Sophia was turned into a Mohammedan mosque. For some centuries the link between the Latin and Greek churches had been growing weaker. Now, with the Turks occupying Greece and Constantinople, these links were completely broken. The Churches of the Byzantine tradition, who called themselves the Orthodox Churches, went their way in isolation from Rome and the western world.

Within the western Church there were also signs of disquiet. The Christian kings and emperors professed loyalty to the Church but often used it for their own selfish ends. They were especially tempted by the wealth which many of the cathedrals and monasteries had acquired, and they often succeeded in having their own supporters appointed bishops or abbots. The result was that many leading churchmen were more interested in money than in religion and were servants of the king rather than of God.

There were good people who protested against this as a betrayal of the teaching of Christ. Some of these, like Francis of Assisi, tried to reform the Church from within and purify it from its human defects. Others rejected the Church outright and wanted to go back to what they said was the true Christianity, before it had been corrupted by Rome. Since some of the things they said ran counter to the official teaching of the Church, they were regarded as heretics.

The Church set up the Inquisition to deal with these heretics. The consequences were tragic. In theory, the Inquisition was meant to win back the heretic to the truth and only to use force when all other means had failed. In practice, the Inquisition became an instrument of oppression and was used by kings and governments to get rid of their political opponents. There were many notorious cases of injustice, such as the burning of Joan of Arc in 1431, allegedly for witchcraft and heresy but in reality because she had defeated the English in several battles. The treacherous execution of John Huss in 1415 and the excesses of the Spanish Inquisition were other blots upon the history of these times.

Many of the so-called heretics were sincere men and women who were pointing out real defects in the Church of Christ. The policy of persecuting them was both unjust and ineffective. As long as there were abuses in the Church people would continue to protest against them; and the way to stop the protests was to correct the abuses and not to torture and kill the protesters. The failure of the Church of the late Middle Ages to root out corruption prepared the way for the Protestant Reformation.

Yet the fifteenth century had its claims to glory also. One of them was a small book written in Holland early in the century, probably by a priest called Thomas a Kempis. The book was written in Latin and its title was *The Imitation of Christ*.

Apart from the Bible, no other Christian book has been so widely printed and translated and read as *The Imitation of Christ*. It is a practical book with a practical aim: to make the reader more like Jesus Christ. It is written in short, pithy sentences, more a collection of sayings than a continuous treatise. One can open it at any page and find a thought that strikes right to one's heart. One can dip into it at any time with the certainty that it will have something of value to say.

It is not a book for intellectuals only. In fact, the author is critical of those intellectuals who talk and write about religion but do not practise it, as he makes clear in the very first chapter:

Right:

Joan of Arc by Ingres (1780-1867), a typical example of nineteenth century religious art. The details of costume and armour are carefully researched but the over-all impression is false and sentimental.

84

What does it profit you to dispute deeply about the Trinity, if you are lacking in humility and so are displeasing to the Trinity?

In truth, sublime words do not make a saint and a just man; but a virtuous life makes one dear to God.

I would rather feel compunction than know its definition.

If you knew the whole Bible and the sayings of all the philosophers, what would it profit you without charity and the grace of God?

Vanity of vanities and all is vanity, save to love God and serve him alone.

The book clearly reflects the time in which it was written, a time when many Christians were becoming lukewarm and when clergy and religious were losing their fervour. The author speaks sternly to religious who went about too freely: "Often a joyful going out results in a sorrowful homecoming, and many a merry evening makes a sad morning." Again, he reflects the current attitude to Holy Communion when he expresses the wish that people would be worthy to communicate every day "if it could be done without attracting attention." But the essential message of the book, that the love and service of God is all that matters in the long run, is as relevant to the twentieth century as it was to the fifteenth.

Give me, O most sweet and loving Jesus, to repose in you above all things created;
above all health and beauty;
above all glory and honour;
above all power and dignity;
above all knowledge and subtlety;
above all riches and arts;
above all joy and gladness;
above all fame and praise;
above all sweetness and consolation;
above all hope and promise;
above all merit and desire;
above all gifts and presents that you can give and infuse;
above all joy and jubilation that the mind can contain or feel;
above all angels and archangels and all the host of heaven;
above all things visible and invisible;
above everything that is not you, my God;
for you, O Lord my God, are supremely good above all things.

The Middle Ages are sometimes looked on as a time when human progress was held back by the influence of the Church. Nothing could be further from the truth. It was the Church which kept civilisation alive during the Dark Ages and re-established it during the Middle Ages. The mediaeval Church gave us Gothic architecture, the most exalted of all architectural styles. It revived the art of sculpture and created the art of stained glass. It laid the foundations of the art of music and opened the way to the masterpieces of later centuries. It rediscovered drama and the theatre and used them for the glory of God. It developed education, from the humble parish school to the great university. It inspired the growth of a new spirit in painting and in poetry and in philosophy. If the mediaeval Church suffered a decline towards the end of the period, this cannot take away from the glory of its greatest achievements.

CHAPTER FIVE

RENAISSANCE AND REFORMATION

There were two movements which put an end to what we call the Middle Ages. These were the Reformation and the Renaissance. The beginning of the Reformation can be dated quite precisely to October 31, 1517. The Renaissance began earlier and more gradually.

The word Renaissance means rebirth and it refers to the renewed interest in the culture of ancient Greece and Rome that developed in Italy during the course of the fifteenth century. The men of the Middle Ages were by no means unaware of the literature of the past: we have already seen how Thomas Aquinas was influenced by Aristotle, and Dante by Virgil. But they were not obsessed with antiquity in the way the men of the Renaissance were.

The men of the Renaissance were not interested merely in the literature of Greece and Rome but in their whole civilisation and way of life. They looked on the Middle Ages as no more than a continuation of the Dark Ages, and they regarded mediaeval literature and art and architecture as not far removed from barbarism. It was only by going back to the period before the coming of the barbarians that true civilisation could be re-established.

The works of the principal writers of Greece and Rome were published in scholarly new editions; this was made possible by the invention of the printing press around 1450, which meant that books no longer had to be copied out by hand. Ancient buildings were measured and studied and a new style of architecture was evolved which imitated them and used such features as classical pillars supporting triangular pediments. The surviving Greek and Roman statues were used as models for new works and the art of sculpture regained its independence; a statue was now looked on as an object in its own right, not just as a decoration for a building. Hardly any ancient paintings had survived but the Renaissance painters paid their tribute to the past by using legends about the ancient gods as subjects for their pictures. Venus and Mars figured alongside scenes from the Gospels in the sketch-books of painters and sculptors.

A spirit of paganism began to spread among artists and among the patrons for whom they worked. These included some Popes and cardinals, who were among the most generous of the patrons and who attracted Italy's leading artists to Rome. The churchmen who ordered naked gods and goddesses to be painted all over the walls and ceilings of their apartments were not always models of Christian living. Many of them led worldly and dissolute lives, among them the notorious Alexander VI who was Pope from 1492 to 1503 and who was the father of the even more notorious Caesar and Lucretia Borgia. At a time when the Church was in sore need of reform, the leaders of the Church seemed more in love with pagan beauty than with Christian truth.

Yet this was the place and the time which was to produce some of the greatest religious art ever created. The period from 1500 to 1520 approximately is often called the High Renaissance and it is the period when Michelangelo and Raphael were both working in Rome. These two, together with Leonardo da Vinci, enjoyed a fame during their own life-times which few other artists have ever achieved.

The dignity of Christian death shines through this detail from El Greco's **Burial of Count Orgaz.**

The High Renaissance

The oldest of the three was Leonardo da Vinci (1452-1519), a man of universal genius who was as much interested in science and engineering and medicine as he was in art. He pursued so many projects that he had time to finish few. His small output of paintings includes one of the *Last Supper,* which he painted on the wall of a refectory in Milan shortly before 1500. It shows Jesus and the twelve apostles seated at a long table, each with his own distinct personality as he reacts to the words, "One of you is about to betray me," yet all welded together into a harmonious whole. Although the painting has flaked and faded badly, it is so masterly in conception that it has eclipsed every other painting of the same subject. When one thinks of the Last Supper, one thinks automatically of Leonardo's picture of it. The two have become inseparable.

Michelangelo Buonarotti (1475-1564) was also a man of wide-ranging genius but unlike Leonardo he left behind a body of completed work which shows his talents in their full magnificence. He was a brilliant architect, he wrote splendid poetry, he carved statues that throbbed with life, he painted like an angel. His contemporaries called him the divine Michelangelo. He himself believed that his works owed their beauty to God and not to himself: the statue lay hidden in the block of marble and all the artist did was to cut away

The Last Supper, by Leonardo da Vinci. The artist tried a new method of painting with oil directly on to the wall which did not work, and so the picture has deteriorated badly.

the stone shell that enclosed it. He wrote in one of his sonnets:

The best of artists hath no thought to show
Which the rough stone in its superfluous shell
Doth not include: to break the marble spell
Is all the hand that serves the brain can do.

The masterpiece which first made him famous was his *Pietà*, a larger than lifesize sculpture of the dead Christ resting on his mother's lap. The technical problems were considerable: in order to balance the group, the figure of the Blessed Virgin had to be massive enough to support the body of Christ yet must not appear heavy or unfeminine. Not only did

Michelangelo achieve this seeming impossibility, he also gave to her face an expression of tenderness and restrained grief that is intensely moving.

In 1508 he was commissioned to decorate the ceiling of the Sistine Chapel in Rome, the private chapel of the Pope. He was allowed to choose his own subjects, a rare tribute to his abilities. For the next four years he was to spend most of his time lying on his back on top of a sixty-foot-high scaffold, adding figure after figure and scene after scene to the immense composition, while the paint dripped down his brush on to his hands and face and his whole body was racked with cramp.

One could spend a lifetime studying this vast panorama of Creation and Prophecy without exhausting its meaning. The artist reached his sublimest heights in showing the creation of man, where the outstretched finger of God imparting life reaches out to meet the outstretched finger of Adam receiving it. One's eye follows the current of creation along the two arms to the head of Adam as he looks at his Creator in wonder and gratitude. This is man before the fall; in spite of his superbly modelled body, he is as innocent and as vulnerable as a child.

As he grew older, Michelangelo's attitude to his art became more and more deeply spiritual. "In order to copy to some extent the sacred likeness of our Lord," he told a friend, "it is not enough to have great mastery of painting and great wisdom. I think it is also necessary for the painter to be a very good-living man or even if possible a saint, so that the Holy Spirit may inspire his soul."

In 1536 he was persuaded to return to the Sistine Chapel and paint a fresco of the *Last Judgment* on the huge wall above the altar. By this time he was a changed man, saddened and shaken by two recent tragic events, the Lutheran revolt and the sack of Rome. His style had lost its earlier serenity and had become more tense and emotional, the style which later became known as Mannerism. The *Last Judgment* is a powerful and disturbing work, full of bodies in restless motion. The only point of repose is the figure of Christ the Judge, magnificent in its majesty.

Michelangelo lived to be almost ninety. He worked up to the end, although in his last years his art could no longer satisfy the yearning of his great soul for God. In one of his late sonnets he wrote:

Now hath my life across a stormy sea,
Like a frail bark, reached the wide port where all
Are bidden, ere the final reckoning fall
Of good and evil for eternity.

Now well I know how that fond fantasy
Which made my soul the worshipper and thrall
Of earthly art is vain; how criminal
Is that which all men seek unwillingly.

Those amorous thoughts which were so lightly dressed,
What are they when the double death is nigh?
The one I know for sure, the other dread.
Painting nor sculpture now can lull to rest
My soul, that turns to his great love on high
Whose arms to clasp us on the cross were spread.

He was working on another *Pietà* when his final illness

Right:

Pietà by Michelangelo. This group is now in a side chapel of St Peter's Basilica in Rome.

92

came upon him. He died a few days later, on February 18, 1564, and that heart which had sought beauty for so many years was at last granted its desire.

In contrast to Michelangelo, Raffaello Sanzio or Raphael (1483-1520) had a life as smooth and effortless as his painting, and the only tragedy to touch him was his early death. His finest work was a series of frescoes in the Pope's apartments, but he is better known to most people as the painter of many charming pictures of our Lady (Madonna in Italian). Some of these were easel paintings, that is to say, they were painted in the artist's studio on wood or canvas and not directly on to a wall. Though Raphael did not invent the easel painting, he helped to make it popular. Nowadays paintings which can be moved from place to place are the rule rather than the exception.

A typical Raphael painting is the well-known *Madonna of the Chair*. The mother and child are fitted into a circular frame, from which both look out towards the spectator. They have the appearance of an Italian peasant family, human and approachable; there is nothing in the least awe-inspiring about them. There is a gain but also a loss: the humanity is emphasised by playing down the supernatural. If Fra Angelico was a saint and Michelangelo a would-be saint, then Raphael was no more than a superbly gifted artist.

Raphael was easier to imitate than Michelangelo and his influence is traceable in religious art down to the present day, not always with the happiest results. Artists who came after him found it commercially profitable to copy his unassuming style, though without his unfailing good taste. The sentimental Madonnas and simpering Infants of later centuries can trace their ancestry back to the Roman studio of Raffaello Sanzio.

One great project which started in Rome in the time of Raphael and Michelangelo and which involved both of them was the building of the new St Peter's. The old basilica built in the time of the Emperor Constantine was now over a thousand years old and in danger of falling down. Instead of repairing it, the decision was made to knock it all down and build a new basilica which would be the largest and finest church in the world. After a number of false starts, the work finally got under way in 1506 under the supervision of the brilliant architect, Donato Bramante. His design was for an enormous church in the form of a Greek cross (a cross whose four arms are all of equal length) with a splendid dome over the crossing. A greater contrast with the Gothic type of church would be difficult to

imagine.

The building of St Peter's was to go on for a hundred and twenty years and to involve many changes of plan. When Bramante died in 1514, Raphael was appointed chief architect until his own death in 1520. Raphael altered the plan to make the nave longer than the other three arms, the shape known as the Latin cross. Michelangelo accepted the job in 1546 and revised the plans again; he went back to the Greek cross and strengthened the piers in the church to support an even more magnificent dome than Bramante's. After his death several other architects continued the work, which was finally completed by Carlo Maderna. The Maderna design left Michelangelo's dome unchanged but lengthened the nave to form a Latin cross and finished the front of the building with a rather dull facade.

The church was consecrated at last in 1626. It was and still is the largest in the world. Its chief glory is the dome of Michelangelo, equally impressive when viewed from the inside or from the outside, a marvel of engineering as well as of art. The interior is of the greatest magnificence, with a gilded barrel-vaulted ceiling and marble walls and pillars. The whole

The Creation of Adam by Michelangelo, one of the scenes depicted on the ceiling of the Sistine Chapel in Rome.

95

impression is one of overwhelming richness, a perfect setting for great occasions and elaborate ceremonial. There are some, however, who have found fault with it as lacking the prayerful and spiritual atmosphere of a Gothic cathedral and have seen in it a monument to the glory of the men who built it as much as to the God for whom it was built.

Martin Luther

The whole of Christendom was called upon to give money for the building of St Peter's. Preachers were sent around Europe proclaiming that a contribution to the building fund was a good deed which would earn the giver an indulgence, that is, a lessening of the punishment to be suffered in Purgatory. Some of these preachers offended many people by their crude and money-grabbing approach. While it was reasonable to describe almsgiving as a good deed which would be looked on favourably by God, it was wrong to suggest that God's favour could be bought or sold like any commercial product.

One of those who protested against this kind of preaching was a young German Augustinian called Martin Luther (1483-1546). On October 31, 1517, he nailed a document to the church door at Wittenberg which attacked the whole doctrine of indulgences. That simple action marked the beginning of the Protestant Reformation.

There were many others all over Europe who were dissatisfied with the Church at that time. All they needed was a leader and they found one in Martin Luther. Within five years the whole of Germany was in turmoil as the smouldering complaints and frustrations of centuries suddenly burst into flame. The savagery of Luther's attacks, the power of the sermons he preached and even more of the pamphlets he wrote, the truth of many of the accusations he made against the leaders of the Church, all combined to win increasing numbers to his side and away from Rome. What began as a movement to reform the Church quickly became a Church of its own, which claimed to be the true Church as Jesus himself wanted it to be.

Many of the traditional beliefs and practices were swept away: the sacrifice of the Mass, praying to the saints, obedience to the Pope, confession of sins, acceptance of the teaching authority of the Church, among many others. Lutheranism spread throughout northern Germany and Scandinavia while other forms of Protestantism took root elsewhere in, Europe. Calvinism, taking its name from the Frenchman John

Left:

Virgin and Child with St John by Raphael, generally known as the Madonna of the Chair.

Interior of St Peter's Basilica in Rome, looking from the main entrance towards the high altar.

Calvin, spread from Switzerland and became the dominant religion in Holland and Scotland. In England, Henry VIII declared that the Church of England was independent of the Church of Rome and so laid the foundations for Anglicanism. By 1560 the unity of Christendom was at an end. Henceforth there would be two Christian traditions in western Europe, the Catholic tradition and the Protestant or Reformed tradition.

Luther set the seal of his own personality upon the whole of the Protestant tradition, both for good and for ill. The Bible for him was the one teaching authority and he made it the centre of every Protestant home. He translated it into clear and forceful German, and though his was not the first German translation it was the first to be widely circulated and read. Copies of Luther's Bible poured from the printing presses and were eagerly bought by those for whom the old Latin translation was a closed book. His German Bible was a landmark both in the history of religion and in the development of German literature.

A second contribution he made was in the reorganisation of worship. He saw clearly the need to break down the barriers between the altar and the

people. He allowed them to receive communion under the forms of both bread and wine and he produced a new version of the Mass in the German language. Since he did not accept that the Mass was a sacrifice, he left out most of the Eucharistic Prayer and gave greater prominence to the scripture readings and to the sermon. This German Mass was rejected by the Catholic Church authorities, not because of the language but because its idea of the meaning of the Mass ran against the traditional Catholic teaching.

A third and very important contribution made by Luther to the Christian heritage was in the field of music. He was a lover of music and a firm believer in its power. "Next to the Word of God," he said, "only music deserves to be extolled as the mistress and governess of the feelings of the human heart." He published collections of hymns or chorales for congregations to sing, with German words and simple tunes. He wrote the words of many of them himself and may have written some of the tunes also. They were something quite new and became immensely

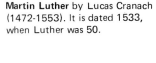

Martin Luther by Lucas Cranach (1472-1553). It is dated 1533, when Luther was 50.

popular, being sold like ballad sheets in the streets of the German cities. "Luther killed more souls with his hymns than with his sermons," said one of his opponents.

Luther's attitude to the other arts was much less favourable. He was indifferent to religious architecture and hostile to religious painting and sculpture. Since he did not believe in the intercession of the saints, he was opposed to having their images in church buildings. Some of his followers rivalled the iconoclasts of old in their enthusiastic smashing of statues and burning of pictures. A full century after Luther's death, Cromwell's soldiers in England and Ireland were still destroying works of art in the name of the true religion.

The tragedy of Martin Luther is that his great gifts should have led to such deep divisions. Christians became divided into Catholics and Protestants, each unable to see what was good in the others' traditions. Religious art died in the Protestant countries, because it was associated with Catholic beliefs and practices. Mass in the language of the people was forbidden in the Catholic countries, because it was linked with Protestant theology. It took centuries for emotions to cool and for people to judge ideas for themselves and not for the Catholic or Protestant labels attached to them.

The Founding of the Jesuits

Martin Luther was one of the two men who shaped the religious history of the sixteenth century. The other was Ignatius of Loyola.

Ignatius was born at Loyola in Spain in 1491, eight years after the birth of Luther. He became a soldier and at the age of thirty was commander of the garrison in the town of Pamplona when it was besieged by the French. He suffered a severe leg wound which led to several extremely painful operations and left him with a permanent limp. While recovering from the wound he read all the novels he could lay his hands on, and when these were finished he had nothing to fall back on except some lives of Christ and the saints. To his surprise he found himself deeply moved by them and a resolution began to form in his mind. As a cripple he could no longer serve in the army of the king, but there was nothing to prevent him from spending the rest of his life in the service of the King of Kings.

He spent a year in the town of Manresa, much of the time in a dark cave, a year of silence and prayer and planning. Then he started to repair the gaps in his

St Ignatius of Loyola, a print
based on a painting by Rubens.

education, finishing up in 1534 with the degree of
Master of Arts at the University of Paris. In Paris he
gathered around him a small group of men who shared
his ideals and were fired with his enthusiasm, among
them a fellow Spaniard called Francis Xavier. They
made their way to Rome and placed themselves at the
service of the Pope, who was quick to recognise their
qualities.In 1540 he approved of them as a religious
order under the name of the Society of Jesus and the
following year Ignatius was elected their first General.

The growth of the Jesuits, as members of the Society
were called, was almost as spectacular as the growth of
the Franciscans and a good deal better organised. The
title of General was an appropriate one for Ignatius the
ex-soldier, since he ran the Society like an army and
expected strict discipline and unquestioning obedience
from his men. He wrote a kind of training manual for
them which he based on his experiences in the cave at
Manresa and called *The Spiritual Exercises*. It was a
short book but a deeply influential one and it helped to
form the Jesuits into the most effective force that the
Pope had at his disposal. For the next two centuries the

101

history of the Catholic Church was to a large extent the history of the Society of Jesus.

St Ignatius's *Spiritual Exercises* have little or no value as literature. The book is a practical manual, a series of guidelines and instructions, a do-it-yourself handbook of the spiritual life. If we compare it with *The Imitation of Christ* we find that the aim is the same but the method completely different. While the *Imitation* moves us by its inspiring thoughts and language, the *Exercises* give us cold logic and facts. It begins with a stark statement of the Fundamental Principle which should govern our attitude to God:

> Man has been created to praise, reverence and serve our Lord God, thereby saving his soul.
>
> Everything else on earth has been created for man's sake, to help him to achieve the purpose for which he has been created.
>
> So it follows that man has to use them as far as they help and abstain from them where they hinder his purpose.
>
> Therefore we need to train ourselves to be impartial in our attitudes towards all created reality, provided that we are at liberty to do so, that is to say that it is not forbidden. So that, as far as we are concerned, we do not set our hearts on good health as against bad health, prosperity as against poverty, a good reputation as against a bad one, a long life as against a short one, and so on.
>
> The one thing we desire, the one thing we choose, is what is more likely to achieve the purpose of our creating.

The book is not meant to be read through but to be lived through. It provides the material for a retreat of four weeks, leading the reader from repentance of his sins in the first week to close union with God in the last. In between it has methodical advice on mental prayer, examination of conscience, self-control, scruples and so on. There is an important section in the third week telling how to make a decision correctly, particularly a decision regarding one's career in life. If many of those who followed the *Exercises* decided at this point to become Jesuits, they were accepting the logical consequences of the Fundamental Principle.

Ignatius recommended that anyone who wanted to make the *Exercises* properly should do so under the guidance of a qualified director, should set aside a month for the purpose, and should go to live in some place where he would be free from all distractions. He

Right:

St Teresa in Ecstasy by Bernini, in the Church of S. Maria della Vittoria in Rome.

Giovanni Pierluigi da Palestrina.

recognised that these things were not always possible, especially for lay people, and was prepared to compromise on the details. From this began the custom for lay people to make a few days' retreat occasionally, either by going to live in a religious house or else by visiting a church every evening after work for prayer and instruction. The *Spiritual Exercises* not only formed a corps of dedicated Jesuits but also influenced many other clergy and layfolk and brought about a much needed spiritual renewal throughout the Church.

The ink was hardly dry on the Pope's Bull of Approval when Jesuits seemed to be appearing all over the world. Two Jesuits were sent to Ireland in 1541 to make a report for the Pope on Catholic resistance to the policy of Henry VIII. In the same year, Francis Xavier left for the Far East, which had recently been opened up by Portuguese explorers, and swept like a tornado through India, Ceylon, Malaya and Japan. In Germany and Poland Jesuits won back for the Catholic Church large areas which had seemed firmly Protestant a short while before. Jesuit schools and colleges were set up throughout Italy, France, Spain and Portugal. Ignatius remained all the time in Rome, planning and directing operations, and saw the Society growing until there were a thousand Jesuits at work in Europe, Africa, Asia, and the newly discovered continent of America.

By the end of the century their number had grown to about 10,000 and their influence had grown even faster. The long spiritual and intellectual training which they received before being admitted to the priesthood fitted them to become leaders of men. Popes relied on them for the most difficult tasks, kings called on them for spiritual and even political advice, universities sought them as lecturers and professors. In the mission fields they blazed the trails that others were to follow. In the Catholic countries of Europe they moulded successive generations of boys in their schools. They were the mainspring behind the movement which reformed the Catholic Church in the sixteenth century, the movement which is sometimes called the Catholic Reformation or more often the Counter-Reformation.

Ignatius of Loyola died on June 2, 1556, ten years after Martin Luther. He is remembered as a man utterly dedicated to his ideals, who could ask and obtain the same dedication from others. A phrase he constantly used was *Ad majorem Dei gloriam* (For the greater glory of God) and his life had room for no other ambition.

Reformers and Mystics

In order to make the Counter-Reformation effective, it was necessary to hold a General Council of the Church. There was no point in issuing decrees from Rome if they were ignored by local bishops. The only solution was to invite all the bishops to a council of reform and so involve them in the decision-making process. This would at the same time give an opportunity of re-examining some points of doctrine that had been attacked by the Protestants.

It took Pope Paul III ten years to get the council together. In 1536 he announced that it would be held in Mantua the following year but nobody took any notice. He tried again, this time at Vicenza, and only five bishops turned up. The Germans would not go to Italy, the Italians would not go to Germany. Finally the little border town of Trent was chosen as a compromise and the Council opened there on December 13, 1545. It lasted on and off until 1563.

From the beginning the Council of Trent concerned itself with both doctrine and discipline: that is, it restated the truths of Christian belief and at the same time passed decrees dealing with the reformation of Church life. In the field of doctrine, it dealt with such subjects as original sin, the Mass and the sacraments in a firm and balanced manner. The language it used,

William Byrd.

however, is the language of the sixteenth century and is therefore sometimes open to misunderstanding today.

In the field of discipline, the Council made a number of far-reaching regulations, particularly with regard to the clergy. It renewed the laws forbidding priests to marry (the Protestants had allowed them to marry), it laid down the duties of bishops and parish priests, and it recommended the setting up of seminaries in which future priests could receive a suitable training. It dealt at length with the reform of the religious orders and called on their members to be faithful to their vows and to the religious rules.

All this could have remained a dead letter if it had not received the backing of the cardinals, bishops and religious superiors. When they returned home, they started the first genuine effort to reform the Church from within that had been made for three centuries. The setting up of seminaries brought about a rapid improvement in the quality of the clergy. The reforms of the religious orders of men and women brought them back to the ideals of their founders and gave them new life.

Among the reformers of religious orders, the most remarkable were a rather ill-assorted Spanish couple: a stoutish middle-aged nun and a very small, very intense young friar. Despite appearances, there was much in common between Teresa of Avila (1515-1582) and John of the Cross (1542-1591). Both were

Carmelites, both were mystics, both were writers of genius. St Teresa of Avila has only one equal in the whole of mystical literature and that is St John of the Cross.

Mysticism is not something that originated in sixteenth-century Spain. It has been found in all the centuries of Christianity and in religions besides Christianity. The point at which ordinary prayer becomes mystical prayer is not easy to define but it is roughly the point at which we stop using our own efforts and something or someone else takes over. When we are praying by our own efforts, says St Teresa, we are like a fledgling bird making repeated efforts to rise into the air:

> Then, as one stage succeeds another, the Lord takes up this small bird and puts it into the nest where it may be quiet. He has watched it fluttering for a long time, trying with its understanding and its will and all its strength to find God and please him; and now he is pleased to give it its reward in this life. And what a reward! One moment of it is enough to repay all the trials it can ever have endured.

Teresa had been an ordinary kind of nun for more than twenty years before she realised she was called to something higher. Like the other sisters in the

Orlandus Lassus, sometimes called Orlando di Lasso.

Carmelite Convent at Avila, she led a comfortable and undemanding life. Then gradually she found herself being drawn closer to God in prayer and strange things began to happen. Sometimes she fell into a trance, sometimes she was raised above the ground. She had visions of God, of the Blessed Virgin, of different saints. One vision of an angel with a golden spear seemed to symbolise the complete surrender of her soul to God:

> He was not tall but short and very beautiful; and his face was so aflame that he appeared to be one of the highest ranks of angels, who seem to be all on fire. They must be of the kind called Cherubim, but they do not tell me their names. I know very well that there is a great difference between some angels and others, and between these and others still, but I could not possibly explain it.
>
> In his hands I saw a great golden spear, and at the iron tip of it there appeared to be a point of fire. This he plunged into my heart several times so that it penetrated to my entrails. When he pulled it out, I felt that he took them with it, and left me utterly consumed by the great love of God. The pain was so severe that it made me utter several moans.
>
> The sweetness caused by this intense pain is so extreme that one cannot possibly wish it to cease, nor is one's soul then content with anything but God. This is not a physical pain but a spiritual pain, though the body has some share in it — even a considerable share. So gentle is this wooing which takes place between God and the soul that if anyone thinks I am lying, I pray God in his goodness to grant him some experience of it.

As a result of these experiences, Teresa decided to leave her convent and set up another one, where she and a few others could live in accordance with the spirit of the old Carmelite rule. She was 47 at the time. She had twenty more years to live, during which she travelled all over Spain, interviewing candidates, buying houses for new convents, dealing with lawyers and builders and town officials about all kinds of practical details, while at the same time as conscious of God's presence as if he had been standing in front of her. She managed also to write her life story, a history of her convents, two books on prayer, a number of shorter works and innumerable letters.

In 1567 she met John of the Cross, less than five feet in height but with a heart like a lion. Encouraged by her he started a parallel movement to reform the male Carmelite order. What happened next showed how badly reform was needed. He was kidnapped by some Carmelites from Toledo and imprisoned in a windowless cell, from which he was taken out once a day and beaten. He endured almost nine months of this before he managed to escape. He brought with him some poems˙that he had begun to write, the first of many that were to tell of the relationship between the soul and God in terms of a love affair in which the soul is the bride and God the bridegroom.

> Upon a gloomy night,
> With all my cares to loving ardours flushed,
> (O venture of delight!)
> With nobody in sight
> I went abroad when all my house was hushed.
>
> O night that was my guide!
> Oh darkness dearer than the morning's pride,
> Oh night that joined the lover
> To the beloved bride
> Transfiguring them each into the other.
>
> Lost to myself I stayed
> My face upon my lover having laid
> From all endeavour ceasing;
> And all my cares releasing
> Threw them amongst the lilies there to fade.

His poems became very popular and he was often asked to explain them. Eventually, he started to write commentaries on some of the poems and these commentaries grew longer until they formed substantial books. Two of these are based on the poem from which the stanzas just quoted are taken. One of them he called *The Ascent of Mount Carmel* and in it he described how the soul must prepare itself for union with the heavenly bridegroom by putting aside all desire for things of earth:

> In order to arrive at having pleasure in everything, desire to have pleasure in nothing.
> In order to arrive at possessing everything, desire to possess nothing.
> In order to arrive at being everything, desire to be nothing.
> In order to arrive at knowing everything, desire to know nothing.

Many spiritual trials await the soul on its way to the

Beloved and these he described in the second commentary, *The Dark Night of the Soul.* His two remaining works, *The Spiritual Canticle* and *The Living Flame of Love,* speak in so far as it is possible to speak of the soul's ecstasy on being united with the Bridegroom and feeling his touch.

> Oh, gentle touch, that are so delicate and gentle! Say, Word, Son of God, how do you touch the soul so gently and delicately when you are so terrible and powerful?
> Oh blessed, thrice blessed, the soul whom you touch so delicately and gently though you are so terrible and powerful!
> Tell this out to the world. Nay, tell it not out to the world, for the world knows naught of air so gentle and will not feel you because it can neither receive you nor see you. Only they who withdraw from the world and whom you refine shall know you, my God and my life, and behold you when you touch them delicately, since purity corresponds with purity, and thus they shall see you and rejoice in you.

Teresa's vivid prose and John's soaring poetry give them a leading place in Spanish literature. As guides on the journey to the heights of prayer they have no equals in the literature of any country. John of the Cross was declared a Doctor (or Teacher) of the Church in 1926 but Teresa as a woman was not considered eligible for the honour. It was not until 1970 that the same title was conferred on her by Pope Paul VI.

A Golden Age of Music

The new spirit brought about by the Council of Trent showed itself in many other ways. It affected musicians, painters, sculptors and architects, and encouraged them to devote their talents to the service of the Church. In doing so, it inspired some of the greatest masterpieces of European art.

The Council discussed the subject of Church music on several occasions. By this time much fine polyphonic music had been written for the Church in the form of motets and Masses. A motet was the name given to a setting for voices of a short scriptural or devotional text. A Mass was a setting for voices of the six sections of the Mass which were traditionally sung by the choir and whose words remained the same all the year round. These were the *Kyrie* (Lord have mercy), *Gloria* (Glory to God in the highest), *Credo* (I believe), *Sanctus* (Holy, holy, holy), *Benedictus*

The facade of the Church of the Gesu in Rome, which was to serve as the model for churches in many parts of the world.

(Blessed is he who comes), and *Agnus Dei* (Lamb of God).

Many of those attending the Council of Trent objected to polyphonic Church music, not because the people could not join in (that would have been regarded as a Protestant argument) but because the music was too long and elaborate, the words could not be clearly heard, and the melodies were often borrowed from popular songs. They wanted all polyphonic music banned from the Church and only Gregorian chant allowed.

In the end the Council did not forbid polyphonic music but only "impure or lascivious" music. The result was that the fifty years following the Council were to become known as the Golden Age of polyphony and Europe was to produce its first great composers. All of them were Catholics, for the Lutherans were so committed to congregational singing that they did not encourage any music of a more elaborate nature.

First and foremost of these was Giovanni Pierluigi da Palestrina (1525-1594), an Italian who worked all his life in Rome. It was believed for many years that his beautiful *Mass of Pope Marcellus (Missa Papae Marcelli)* was sung at Trent and that it persuaded the Council at the last moment not to forbid polyphony;

but this charming story is now known to be untrue. Still, his influence as Rome's leading musician was immense and his Masses were printed and widely performed and imitated. The purity and nobility of his style reflected his deep faith and his music is still regarded as the most perfect ever written for the Roman rite.

His great rival was Orlandus Lassus (1532-1594) who was born in Flanders but spent most of his life in Bavaria. His music does not have the serenity of Palestrina's but it shows greater psychological penetration, and he was always able to find the music to express the exact feeling of a motet, whether joy or sorrow or penance or adoration.

Spain contributed Tomás Luis de Victoria (c. 1540-1611). Victoria was born at Avila and ordained priest around 1565. He spent a long period in Rome before returning to Spain for the last years of his life. He may well have known St Teresa personally and he was certainly at home in the world of Spanish mysticism. At one time he seriously thought of giving up music altogether so as to devote himself more fully to prayer. There is a passionate intensity in his music which suggests that he had experienced the dark night of the soul. In particular, the music he wrote for the offices of Holy Week touches the heart with its feeling of grief and desolation. In all his long life he never wrote a single bar of secular music. His art was for God alone.

The last and the saddest of these great men was William Byrd (1543-1623). He was one of those Englishmen who never accepted the Reformation. In his will, written shortly before his death, he asked God's grace "that I may live and die a perfect member of his Holy Catholic Church". He wrote much beautiful music for the Anglican Church, which was more sympathetic to polyphony than the Lutherans, but he kept his finest inspiration for his own religion. He wrote motets and Masses for a rite that could only be held in secret and behind locked doors. The *Mass for Five Voices*, his last Mass, ends with an *Agnus Dei* of heartbreaking loveliness, as though he knew he was bidding farewell not just to this piece of music but to a whole era.

The music of these and other polyphonic masters may sound austere and colourless to modern ears, because of its restricted range of harmonies and its lack of any instrumental accompaniment. When one comes to know it better, as one can through gramophone records, one enters into a world of unexpected beauty and variety. It can only be fully appreciated, however, when heard in its proper setting as part of an act of divine worship. The voices merge and mingle and the melodies interweave in a mysterious counterpoint, that hardly seems to belong any longer to this world.

The beginning of the Baroque Period

The attitude of the Council of Trent towards painting and sculpture was akin to its attitude towards music: approval and encouragement, but with a warning against anything profane. "All lasciviousness is to be avoided," it said, " and the images of the saints are not to be painted or adorned with beauty of an improper nature." In other words, an end was to be put to the pagan spirit which had shown itself in religious art during the Renaissance.

On the whole this decree was faithfully obeyed by churchmen and artists of the time. In order to set a lead, the Pope decided to have draperies painted on the nude figures in Michelangelo's *Last Judgment*, which was right over the Papal altar in the Sistine Chapel. A talented young Greek artist named Domenikos Theotokopoulos (1541-1614) who was living in Rome at the time suggested that the picture be destroyed and offered to paint a better one in its place. This arrogance caused so much indignation among Roman art lovers

Interior of the Church of the Gesù in Rome. The abolition of side aisles gives a feeling of unity and concentrates attention on the high altar.

that the young man had to leave the city, while another artist undertook the cover-up operation.

The young man was to spend the rest of his life in Spain and become the greatest artist of the Counter-Reformation. The Spaniards could not remember his name so they simply called him El Greco (The Greek). Teresa and John of the Cross were still alive when he began working in Toledo and their influence is clearly to be seen in his strange and mystical paintings.

Apart from portraits, almost all his pictures are on religious subjects, and the saints who appear in them are more like living flames than people of flesh and blood. Their bodies are drawn out to an unnatural height as if striving towards heaven and they seem to be without weight or solidity. Their large soulful eyes are fixed on eternity.

Often the same picture shows both heaven and earth, as in the magnificent *Burial of Count Orgaz*. Below, the body of the dead nobleman is being laid in the tomb, surrounded by clergy and dignitaries; above, the sky is opened and his soul is received by Christ and his mother and a whole multitude of angels and saints. If it is possible to express mysticism in art, then El Greco more than any other artist has done so.

His genius inspired three generations of Spanish painters, among whom were Velasquez and Murillo, and ushered in the greatest century of Spanish art. Right up to his death, though, he never changed his opinion of Michelangelo. "He was a good man," he told a visitor, "but he could not paint."

In the Spanish Netherlands, the immensely gifted Peter Paul Rubens (1577-1640) became the most successful painter of his day and his large output included many religious paintings. Further north, in Holland, Rembrandt van Rijn (1606-1669) was the one important Protestant religious artist of the period. Rembrandt's paintings and engravings of biblical scenes are less showy than those of Rubens but they are more deeply felt.

Italy produced some distinguished painters during the Counter-Reformation, including the long-lived Titian (1487?-1576) and the short-lived Caravaggio (1573-1610), but its most important contributions were to architecture and to sculpture. The most influential new church built in this period was not St Peter's, since St Peter's was on too vast a scale to be imitated. It was the first Jesuit church in Rome, dedicated to the name of Jesus, in Italian *Gesù*.

St Ignatius in his *Spiritual Exercises* gave a number of rules for thinking in accordance with the Church.

St Peter's Square in Rome.
The photograph shows the dome
designed by Michelangelo, the
facade designed by Maderna, and
the semi-circular colonnades
designed by Bernini.

One of them was: "We should praise church decoration and architecture, as well as statues, which we should venerate in view of what they portray." After his death, the Jesuits in Rome began to plan a church which was to be a model of decoration and architecture for Jesuit churches throughout the world. Michelangelo was among several architects involved in the project but he was dead before the start of the building operations, which took place from 1568 to 1584. The decoration of the interior was not completed until a hundred years later.

The most striking feature was that it made the interior of the church into a single space, dominated by the high altar. There were no pillars to break up the space and no side aisles, though there were some small side chapels opening off the nave and containing altars to the saints. The front or facade of the Gesù was equally unusual and equally widely imitated. It consisted of two storeys ornamented with pillars and pilasters, the lower one wider than the upper. The upper storey had a triangular pediment on top and was linked to the lower storey on either side by curving scrolls.

The Gesù was the forerunner of a new style of architecture, the Baroque style. Once they had got away from the rigid nave-and-aisles format, architects were left with a single space which they could shape in all kinds of interesting ways. The Gesù had the shape of a Latin cross but later churches were more adventurous and had square, rectangular, circular or oval shapes or combinations of these. Even the facades of the churches lost their straight walls and began to curve in unexpected directions. Everything seemed to be in motion.

The decoration of the Baroque churches showed the same delight in the unexpected. Statues were made to look like pictures and pictures like statues. The most important painting in the church was on the ceiling of the nave and was meant to give the spectator the illusion that he was looking up into the sky and seeing hosts of angels and saints from below. Some churches even had a place marked on the floor from which the illusion could be seen to best advantage. It was a test for the ingenuity of the artists who had to paint large numbers of figures from this unusual angle and still avoid ending up with a picture full of feet.

The centre of the Baroque style was Rome and its greatest master was Gianlorenzo Bernini (1598-1680). He was not a painter but he was a brilliant architect and one of the greatest sculptors of all time. During his long career he left the imprint of his talents on every part of the city. Inside St Peter's Basilica he designed the stupendous bronze canopy over the high altar and supported it on four twisting columns. Outside the Basilica, he laid out the unforgettable St Peter's Square and surrounded it by two curving colonnades like two arms stretching out from the great church to embrace the city and the world.

Bernini was a deeply committed Catholic who read the *Imitation of Christ* every day and made a retreat every year in accordance with the *Spiritual Exercises* of St Ignatius. For him the love of God was not a dry dogma but an exciting and overwhelming reality, and that excitement is to be seen in all his works. He shows God visiting men not as a gentle breeze but as a gale-force wind, catching them by surprise and tossing all their garments into swirling motion.

One of his most brilliant pieces is his *St Teresa in Ecstasy*, based on the saint's description of the piercing of her heart by the angel. Bernini here re-established the connection between architecture and sculpture, designing the chapel in which it was placed as well as carving the group. The chapel is arranged so that the light falls directly down upon the upturned face of the saint and this effect is strengthened by gilded metal rays descending from above. The angel is also posed in such a way as to draw our eyes to the figure of Teresa. She is caught in the moment of ecstasy and her face is a marvellous study in mingled pain and joy. Her clothing flows like liquid and her whole being seems to dissolve and melt away as the divine lover takes possession of her soul. It is so expressive that it is almost theatrical. Other Baroque artists who did not have Bernini's taste and control often did become over-theatrical in their striving after effect.

The Baroque style spread throughout Europe but not until after 1650. Outside Italy and Spain, the first half of the century was a time of horror and devastation on a scale that had not been seen since the worst days of the barbarians. The long threatened war between Catholics and Protestants in the German-speaking lands broke out in 1618 and spread to involve Denmark, Sweden, Poland and France. In Ireland, the native Catholics rose in rebellion against the English Protestant settlers in 1641 and established their own government. In England, religious tension between Anglicans and Puritans lay behind the civil war which broke out in 1642.

The Peace of Westphalia in 1648 brought an end to the Thirty Years War. In 1649 the execution of King Charles I finished all resistance to Cromwell and his Puritans in England. He then left for Ireland and by 1650 had put an end to all serious opposition there. The wars of religion were over but poverty and famine and disease lingered on for many years. The chief sufferers, Germany and Ireland, had lost more than half their population. Wolves roamed around the burnt-out farmhouses and the fields were choked with weeds as far as the eye could see. Europe was at peace but it was like the peace of a vast graveyard.

CHAPTER SIX

THE AGE OF REASON

From the end of the Thirty Years War until the beginning of the nineteenth century, France was the leading country in Europe. The man who gave it that position was Louis XIV, who became King of France in 1643 at the age of four and ruled it for an unprecedented 72 years until his death in 1715.

Louis was known as *Le Roi Soleil*, the Sun King, because of the brilliance of his reign. He was no more than average as a soldier or as a statesman or as a Christian or as a man; but he was a great king. He had a genius for kingship, for making himself the centre around which everything else revolved, for imposing the mark of his personality on the country and on the age in which he lived. He surrounded himself with pomp and etiquette, he drew artists and architects and playwrights and preachers to his court, he built royal residences of a splendour undreamt of before. The immense palace of Versailles was meant to show the world the greatness of France and to show France the greatness of the man who ruled it. He said, "I am the State"; and while he never went so far as to say, "I am the Church", he often acted as if he believed it.

Apostle of Charity

The foundation for France's greatness had been laid during the reign of his father, Louis XIII. Among the men of that time was one of the most lovable of all the saints, Vincent de Paul (1580-1660), the little peasant priest whose name has become synonymous with love for the poor. Though his origins were humble and his appearance unimpressive, Vincent had talent and ambition as a young man and he succeeded in getting a position as chaplain at the royal court. But he soon found that he could not enjoy the life of a palace priest while the world outside was full of poverty and ignorance and vice. God was calling him to serve the poor and he could not ignore the call.

His first concern was for the faith of the people who lived in the country districts where priests were few and of low quality. It seemed to Vincent that these places were like foreign missionary countries, so he organised groups of priests to tour these areas and preach "missions" there. Eventually he formed these priests into a congregation which became known as the Vincentians. In addition to preaching missions, they

Louis XIV, a marble bust by Bernini.

founded and ran seminaries throughout France for the proper training of future priests.

In 1635 France entered the Thirty Years War and soon the tragic effects began to show themselves. In the battle areas, the armies were followed everywhere by famine and disease. The rest of the country was overrun by refugees, starving and penniless. Vincent set about organising relief with superhuman energy. He opened hospitals, he founded orphanages, he set up aid centres, he sent wagon-loads of food and clothing to the distressed areas. He begged and borrowed from anyone who had anything to give. He was afraid of no one. "A Queen has no need of jewellery," he said to the Queen of France and made off with her diamonds.

His most valuable helpers in all this work were a group of women, peasants like himself, whom he formed into the Sisters of Charity. Up to this, women who entered religious life spent their time behind convent walls, far from the things of the world. But the Sisters of Charity lived and worked among the poor, visited and fed them in their homes, nursed them in the hospitals. It was a completely new idea of the religious life and an inspired one.

During the last years of his life, while Louis XIV

was still a child, Vincent became almost the uncrowned King of France. The Queen Mother (the lady who had given up her diamonds) was Regent and she turned to him constantly for advice. Stories about him began to turn into legends: how he carried home abandoned babies under his black cloak, how he took the place of a galley slave who collapsed from exhaustion. When he died in 1660 he was mourned throughout Europe. He had given to the modern world the first organised system of social services, and not as something cold and official but made warm and loving by the love of Christ.

Jansenism in France

The France that gave us the warmth of Vincent de Paul also gave us the coldness of Jansenism. Jansenism is often described as a French heresy; but it was actually founded on the teaching of a Dutch bishop, Cornelius Jansen, and it was not so much a heresy as an attitude of mind. Jansen held the gloomy view that the grace of salvation was given to very few people, and his followers developed into a kind of Catholic Puritans, convinced that the world was a deeply sinful place and that most of men's activities were displeasing to God.

The headquarters of the Jansenists was the Convent of Port Royal, near Paris. The nuns there came from some of France's leading families, and their influence spread quickly through the French Church. Antoine Arnauld, brother of one of the nuns, wrote a book in 1643 to oppose the practice of frequent communion which the Jesuits had been encouraging; he said that the Blessed Sacrament was so sacred and men so

The Palace of Versailles near Paris, where Louis XIV held his court.

unworthy that it should be received only rarely and after long preparation. "If this book has done good to a hundred people by making them more reverent towards the sacraments," commented Vincent de Paul, "it must have done harm to more than ten thousand by drawing them away altogether".

The most famous member of the Port Royal circle was Blaise Pascal (1623-1662), who also had a sister in the convent. Pascal was a brilliant young mathematician who was converted from a life of indifference during one extraordinary night of prayer, November 23, 1654. He set to work almost immediately upon the religious writings which were to occupy him for the rest of his short life.

He began by attacking the Jesuits, the favourite target of the Jansenists, in a series of pamphlets called *The Provincial Letters*. The pamphlets complained that the Jesuits were lax in their teaching on sin, that they explained away the commandments of God, that they "put cushions under the elbows of sinners". These letters were not altogether fair to the Jesuits but they were so witty and well-written that everyone in France was soon talking about them.

Pascal then began to plan a much more important book, an *Apologia* which would convince men of the truth of the Christian religion. He was still at work on this when he died in 1662. His friends found that he had left behind him a mass of written material on the

St Vincent de Paul.

subject, pieces of paper of various shapes and sizes pinned together in bundles, ideas for a book that he was never to write. The ideas were so striking that it was decided to publish the bits and pieces just as he had left them. They were given the title *Pensées* or *Thoughts*.

Some of the thoughts run for several pages, others are only a line or two. The order in which to put them is impossible to decide since Pascal himself had not decided it. But it is clear that he intended his arguments to appeal to the heart rather than to the reason. He set out to prove God's existence not from the created world but from the hunger of the human soul. Pascal's *Thoughts* have depth and insight and if they contain any Jansenism it is Jansenism at its most attractive:

The last thing we discover when writing a book is what to put first.

⋆

The heart has its reasons which the reason does not know.

⋆

There is light enough for those who want to see and darkness enough for those who are otherwise inclined.

⋆

Between heaven and hell, there is only life, which is the most fragile thing in the world.

⋆

There is no better proof of human vanity than to consider the causes and effects of love: for the whole universe is changed by it. If Cleopatra's nose had been shorter, the face of the earth would have changed.

The Hanging of the Bandits by Jacques Callot (1592-1635), one of a series of etchings which the artist made to show the horrors of the Thirty Years War.

123

Man is no more than a reed, the feeblest thing in nature; but he is a thinking reed. It is not necessary for the entire universe to take up arms in order to crush him: a vapour, a drop of water is sufficient to kill him. But if the universe crushed him, man would still be nobler than the thing which destroys him because he knows that he is dying; and the universe which has him at its mercy is unaware of it.

★

Man is neither angel nor beast, and unfortunately he who tries to play the angel ends by playing the beast.

★

It is better not to fast and be ashamed than to fast and be complacent.

★

We implore God's mercy not in order that he will leave us to enjoy our vices undisturbed, but in order that he will deliver us from them.

★

'Be comforted. You would not be seeking me if you had not already found me.'

In 1653 the Pope had condemned five propositions taken from the writings of Jansen but this did nothing to end the matter. The Jansenists agreed that the propositions were heretical but said that they were not in fact to be found anywhere in Jansen's works. The arguments continued until 1709 when Louis XIV, who suspected the Jansenists of plotting against him, took drastic action. He closed the convent of Port Royal, sent all the nuns to other convents, and then had the entire building levelled to the ground. But the influence of Jansenism lingered on for many years, weakening the Church in France and giving the impression that religion was a gloomy and joyless affair, an impression that has not yet completely died away.

The King's brutal manner of dealing with the Jansenists was typical of his whole reign. Where the Pope used gentleness, he used force. He treated the French Protestants or Huguenots with great cruelty and many of them had to fly to England and Ireland to avoid his persecution. He tried to run the Catholic Church as if it were a government department, appointing bishops and abbots himself and blocking any attempt by the Pope to intervene. He taxed the people without mercy to pay for his wars and his buildings until the peasants, without a Vincent de Paul

to speak for them, sank into worse poverty than before. The splendours of his reign were based on misery and supported by tyranny.

The other rulers of Europe were not slow to follow the example of the Sun King. Just as they tried to copy the brilliance of his court and the magnificence of his palaces, so they imitated his dictatorial attitude towards his subjects and towards the Church. The eighteenth century was a century of royal despots, empty of talent but full of vanity and self-importance.

Two Nuns of Port Royal by Philippe de Champaigne (1602-1674). The artist painted this in thanksgiving for the recovery from paralysis of his daughter, the young nun on the right.

Puritans and Anglicans

There was only one country in Europe where the king no longer had absolute power, and that was England. The execution of Charles I in 1649 put an end to royal despotism and when his son Charles II returned to the throne in 1660 he had to act with caution. The restoration of the king was a defeat for the Puritans but they were still a force in the land.

It was from the ranks of these defeated Puritans that two of the masterpieces of Christian literature were to come. The seventeenth century in England produced many fine religious poets, some Anglicans, some Catholics, some veering from one Church to the other. But the greatest of them was neither a Catholic nor an Anglican but a Puritan.

125

John Milton (1608-1674) was a wealthy Londoner who gave his enthusiastic support to the struggle against the king and who held the important position of Latin secretary in Cromwell's government. His political activities left him little time for poetry and it was not until after Cromwell's death that he could settle down to write the epic poem which he had been planning for many years. The restoration of the king marked the lowest point of his career. He had been dismissed from his position and imprisoned for a time; his wife and only son had recently died; he had gone completely blind. It was under these circumstances that he wrote what is generally regarded as the greatest poem in the English language, *Paradise Lost*. The poem is in twelve books with a total of more than 10,000 lines and it tells the story of the temptation and fall of Adam and Eve. It has often been compared with Dante's *Divine Comedy:* it has the same vast scale, ranging over Earth, Heaven and Hell, and the same magnificent control of language.

The superb opening books are set in Hell, among the rebel angels who have just been expelled from Heaven. Satan, their leader, resolves to rally them and to resume the war against Heaven:

> What though the field be lost?
> All is not lost; the unconquerable will
> And study of revenge, immortal hate,
> And courage never to submit or yield,
> And what is yet not to be overcome.
> That glory never shall his wrath or might
> Extort from me.

The fallen angels decide to carry on the war by visiting the newly created Earth and winning its inhabitants to their side. Satan himself undertakes the dangerous journey and eventually arrives in the Garden of Paradise. Moved by the beauty of the new world, he falters for a moment, then steels himself again:

> So farewell, hope; and with hope, farewell, fear;
> Farewell remorse; all good to me is lost.
> Evil, be thou my good; by thee at least
> Divided empire with Heaven's King I hold,
> By thee and more than half perhaps will reign,
> As man ere long and this new world shall know.

The Garden of Paradise is described in terms of glowing beauty, the streams, the trees, the animals at peace with one another, the two god-like human beings

Blaise Pascal

who are the first of the human race. Satan overhears them talking about the one tree whose fruit they are forbidden to eat and begins to see how he may bring about their downfall. He leaves them as night begins to fall in Paradise.

> Now came still evening on, and twilight grey
> Had in her sober livery all things clad;
> Silence accompanied, for beast and bird,
> They to their grassy couch, these to their nests
> Were slunk, all but the wakeful nightingale;
> She all night long her amorous descant sung;
> Silence was pleased; now glowed the firmament
> With living sapphires; Hesperus that led
> The starry host rode brightest, till the Moon,
> Rising in clouded majesty, at length
> Apparent queen unveiled her peerless light
> And o'er the dark her silver mantle threw.

Satan's visit to Paradise is seen by God, who sends the angel Raphael to warn Adam and Eve. The warning is in vain. Satan on his return persuades the woman to eat the forbidden fruit and she persuades the man. The poem ends with their expulsion from Paradise into the land of Eden, while a blazing sword and an angel army prevent any hope of a return. But

127

Milton dictating **Paradise Lost** to his daughters by Michael Munkacsy (1844-1900), a nineteenth-century impression of the blind poet composing his masterpiece.

they have been given the promise of a redeemer to come and this hope consoles them as they leave:

> They looking back all the eastern side beheld
> Of Paradise, so late their happy seat,
> Waved over by that flaming brand; the gate
> With dreadful faces thronged and fiery arms.
> Some natural tears they dropped but wiped them
>   soon;
> The world was all before them, where to choose
> Their place of rest, and Providence their guide;
> They hand in hand with wandering steps and slow·
> Through Eden took their solitary way.

As poetry, *Paradise Lost* is beyond criticism. But it is doubtful if Milton achieved the aim he had set before himself at the beginning, which was to "justify the ways of God to man". He makes God into a remote and unappealing figure, and his ways appear mysterious and sometimes even vindictive. On the other hand, Satan is a commanding and even noble personality. There can be little doubt that Milton was unconsciously identifying himself with the fallen angel. Like Satan, he had seen his greatness brought low and his enemies triumphant but he remained proud and defiant to the end. It is an understandable attitude but it is hardly a Christ-like one. *Paradise Lost* is a great

128

The Last Judgment by Michelangelo, a fresco in the Sistine Chapel, Rome. Christ the Judge is seen in the centre with the blessed on his right hand and the damned on his left.

Shrine of St Peter's Chair by Bernini, in St Peter's, Rome. In this baroque masterpiece, the chair is supported by gigantic figures of Saints Augustine, Ambrose, Athanasius and John Chrysostom. The stained glass window represents the Holy Spirit in the form of a dove and is surrounded by gilded angels and rays of light.

poem on a Christian theme rather than a great Christian poem.

A Puritan of a rather different kind was John Bunyan (1628-1688). He too was imprisoned at the time of the Restoration, because he insisted on preaching though he was not a minister of the Anglican Church. Unlike Milton, he came of humble parents and had little education, but this did not prevent him from writing many books and pamphlets. The most famous of these was *The Pilgrim's Progress*, written in 1675 while he was still in jail.

The book is an allegory of human life and it tells of the journey of a man called Christian to the Celestial City. It is a strange mixture of simplicity and shrewdness, of bigotry and charity, of theological argument and vivid adventure. Nevertheless it is one of the most widely read of all books written in English and its places and people have become part of the language: the Slough of Despond, Vanity Fair, Doubting Castle, Giant Despair, Mr Worldly Wiseman, Mr Standfast.

The attraction of the book lies in its ability to turn symbolic figures into people of flesh and blood. A good example is the prudent Mr By-ends who walks part of the way with Christian and his friend Hopeful but then leaves them and joins a more easy-going group:

John Bunyan.

Sir Christopher Wren.

Well, when they had, as I said, thus saluted each other, Mr Money-love said to Mr By-ends, 'Who are they upon the road before us?' (For Christian and Hopeful were yet within view.)

BY-ENDS: 'They are a couple of far countrymen, that after their mode are going on pilgrimage.'
MONEY-LOVE: 'Alas! Why did they not stay, that we might have had their good company? For they and we and you, sir, I hope, are all going on a pilgrimage.'
BY-ENDS: 'We are so, indeed; but the men before us are so rigid, and love so much their own notions, and do also so lightly esteem the opinions of others, that let a man be never so godly yet if he jumps not with them in all things they thrust him quite out of their company.'
SAVE-ALL: 'That is bad, but we read of some that are righteous overmuch; and such men's rigidness prevails with them to judge and condemn all but themselves. But, I pray, what and how many were the things wherein you differed?'
BY-ENDS: 'Why, they in their headstrong manner conclude that it is duty to rush on their journey all

130

weathers; and I am for waiting for wind and tide. They are for hazarding all for God at a clap; and I am for taking all advantages to secure my life and estate. They are for holding their notions though all other men are against them; but I am for religion in what and so far as the times and my safety will bear it. They are for religion when in rags and contempt;

West front of St Paul's Cathedral, London, by Wren. Wren studied in France and he preferred the restrained and dignified style of Louis XIV's architects to the more vigorous Italian Baroque.

131

Voltaire.

Johann Sebastian Bach.

George Frideric Handel.

132

Joseph Haydn.

but I am for him when he walks in his golden slippers, in the sunshine, and in applause.'

After his release from prison, Bunyan added a second part to his book, describing the journey of Christian's wife, Christiana, and her children. It is not as successful as the first part but it has some fine descriptions, among them the passing of Mr Valiant-for-truth through the river of Death to the Celestial City:

Then said he, 'I am going to my Father's; and though with great difficulty I am got hither, yet now do I not repent me of all the trouble I have been at to arrive where I am. My sword I gave to him that shall succeed me in my pilgrimage, and my courage and skill to him that can get it. My marks and scars I carry with me, to be a witness for me, that I have fought his battles who now will be my rewarder.'

When the day that he must go hence was come, many accompanied him to the river side, into which as he went he said, 'Death, where is thy sting?' And as he went down deeper, he said, 'Grave, where is thy victory?' So he passed over, and all the trumpets sounded for him on the other side.

The last sentence is so simple that a child could have written it, yet not even Milton himself has given us anything more beautiful or more moving.

It was during this period that England took the lead in church architecture, owing to an unexpected catastrophe. In France and elsewhere in Europe, the late seventeenth and eighteenth centuries were the era of the great palaces, when all the best architects were employed to glorify the earthly kingdom rather than the heavenly one. The building of churches took second place except in London, where the Great Fire of 1666 created an urgent need and revealed the man who could meet it.

Sir Christopher Wren (1632-1723) was put in charge of the rebuilding of London. Most of the city churches had been destroyed, including the old Gothic St Paul's Cathedral. Wren was faced with a task which would have crushed a lesser man but which inspired him to great heights. He designed more than fifty churches and many other public buildings; among them was his masterpiece, the new St Paul's.

St Paul's is one of the great churches of the world and its dome is worthy to rank beside that of St Peter's. But, like St Peter's, its vastness made it difficult to imitate. Wren's parish churches were more influential

Clement XIV, who suppressed the Jesuits in 1773. He died the following year, it is said of a broken heart.

and were built in a genuinely English style, more restrained than Italian Baroque but not as rigid as the French style favoured by Louis XIV. Their interiors were bright and airy, with large windows and spacious galleries. Outside there was often a classical steeple of a type invented by Wren, in which a number of storeys tapered to a point. This type of design was imitated in many other Anglican churches, not just in London but throughout England and Ireland and in the new American colonies.

Christianity under attack

A new and dangerous heresy began to emerge during the early years of the eighteenth century. It was the movement known as Deism. The Deists believed in God (*Deus* in Latin) in a vague general kind of way, but they regarded Christ as no more than a good man. The various forms of Christianity, Catholic or Protestant, were rejected by them. Man must live not by the words of Scripture or by the teachings of Churches but by reason alone.

They called it the Enlightenment or the Age of Reason. Deism was taken up in the best social circles, where it became fashionable to speak sneeringly of religion and to regard it as something which only the lower classes took seriously. The movement was strong in England and even stronger in France, where it was supported by the writings of Voltaire and Rousseau, and of the scholars who were putting together the first French *Encyclopaedia*. Other countries in those days took their fashions from France, and Deism was among those fashions.

There was a fundamental opposition between the Deists and the absolute monarchs of the time. As reasonable men, the Deists did not believe in the theory of the Divine Right of kings, and it is to their credit that they fought against royal injustice and prepared the way for more democratic government. But Deists and kings were united in one thing, their opposition to the Catholic Church, the Deists because they did not believe in Christianity, the kings because they wanted complete control of everything in their kingdoms.

The target chosen for attack was the Jesuit Order. The Jesuits, who numbered about 22,500 at this time, were still known everywhere for their learning, their dedication, and their utter loyalty to the Pope. If we can destroy the Jesuits, thought the kings, we can control the Church. If we can destroy the Jesuits, thought the Deists, we can destroy the Church.

The first attack on the Jesuits came from Portugal. It was over the Portuguese possession of Paraguay in South America, where Jesuit missionaries were protecting the Indians against the greed and tyranny of the Portuguese authorities. Various accusations were invented against the Jesuits and in 1759 the king signed a decree banishing them from Portugal and from all its colonies. All the Jesuits were rounded up and imprisoned, after which some were deported and others left to die in jail. Their goods and houses were confiscated by the king. The unfortunate Indians in Paraguay rose in revolt to defend the missionaries but were savagely massacred by the Portuguese.

Most of the other Catholic kings followed the example of Portugal by expelling the Jesuits and confiscating their property: the King of France in 1764, the King of Spain and the King of Naples in 1767. They then began to bring pressure upon the Pope to suppress the Order altogether. They threatened to break completely with Rome, as Henry VIII had done, if he did not agree. The unfortunate

135

Clement XIV had no choice but to give in and in 1773 he issued a Brief putting an end to the Order which had been the strongest and loyalest support of the Popes for more than two hundred years.

Individual Jesuits continued to work as secular priests but all their houses, colleges and churches were taken from them. Religious practice and education in Europe were severely affected, and the foreign missions received a setback from which they took many years to recover. The royal despots rejoiced in the way they had humiliated the Pope and reduced the Church to obedience. The Deists rejoiced in the destruction of Christianity which they felt was certain to follow. "Ecrasez l'infâme," Voltaire wrote in one of his letters, "exterminate the pest". It seemed as if he was about to have his wish.

Masterpieces of Music

It is hard to estimate how far the ideas of the Deists affected people outside the upper classes: probably not very much. In Spain, when the king appeared in public he was greeted by shouts of "Give us back the Jesuits!" In Italy two new religious orders were founded, the Redemptorists and the Passionists, and both made rapid progress. In Germany the movement known as Pietism taught a doctrine of simple piety and deepened the faith of many Lutherans. In England John Wesley preached the personal love of Jesus Christ to the poor and uneducated and founded the Methodist Church.

Religious art and architecture continued to decline, for these depended on the patronage of the rich rather than on the faith of the poor. On the other hand, the eighteenth century saw the composition of some of the greatest masterpieces of religious music, especially by composers from the German-speaking lands.

The Lutheran suspicion of choirs had softened as the years passed by. The congregational hymn or chorale was still of great importance but now place was also found for religious cantatas or oratorios, with movements for solo voices or for the choir. Musical instruments had developed, particularly the organ, which was to be found in almost every church. In addition, most towns could muster up a small orchestra of string and wind players to be used in church on festive occasions. Singing without the accompaniment of instruments was now regarded as dull and old-fashioned.

Among the many church musicians of the period the greatest was Johann Sebastian Bach (1685-1750). He was a deeply pious Lutheran, who was content to

Wolfgang Amadeus Mozart.

spend his life as a church organist and choirmaster in various small towns of northern Germany. He drew much of his inspiration from the Lutheran chorales: many of his organ works were based on chorale melodies and his church cantatas always ended with a chorale in which the whole congregation could join. The cantatas show the tender and personal love for Jesus that was characteristic of the Pietists and also a mystical longing for death that seems to have been part of Bach's own religious feeling.

Among his longest works are the Mass in B minor, written for the Catholic ruler of Saxony, and two settings of the Passion of our Lord as described by St John and St Matthew respectively. These three great works are still frequently performed and the *St Matthew Passion* in particular is regarded as one of the highest achievements of Christian art. In it the Gospel story is interrupted from time to time by arias of reflection, choruses of prayer and sorrow, and several repetitions of the chorale "O Sacred Head now wounded", each time to a richer and fuller harmony. To listen to it is a religious as well as a musical experience.

It is a strange thing, then, that the best known and best loved of all the great religious masterworks was not written by the devout Bach but by his more worldly contemporary and rival, George Frideric Handel (1685-1759). Handel was also a north German Lutheran but he was much more interested in making money than Bach and he tried his fortune in different parts of Europe before finally settling in London. For most of his life he was known as a composer of operas and when he decided eventually to change over to religious oratorios it was for financial reasons: his operas were losing money. An oratorio was a lengthy work for voices and instruments, normally using a religious text but not intended to form part of a church service.

In 1741 Handel was invited to come to Dublin and give a series of concerts. He decided to write a new oratorio for the occasion and he began work on the music at his home in London on August 22, 1741. The text consisted of extracts from the Bible and was divided into three parts, dealing with the birth, death, and resurrection of our Lord. It was called *Messiah*.

Handel always worked quickly but this time he seemed to work like a man inspired. Food brought in to him was ignored as he covered page after page of music with his firm clear writing. He finished the first part in seven days, writing music of marvellous joy and tenderness for the shepherds and angels of Bethlehem. Nine days were spent on the second part. The composer wept as he wrote the passion aria "He was despised", and when he came to the Hallelujah Chorus, as he said afterwards, "I did think I did see all heaven before me and the great God himself." Only six days were needed for the third part, opening with the exquisite soprano aria "I know that my Redeemer liveth" and ending with a tremendous fugue on the single word "Amen". Another two days to complete the orchestral part, and then at the end of the score, on page 259, he wrote the date of completion: September 14, 1741.

The first performance of *Messiah* was given at Neal's Music Hall, Fishamble Street, Dublin, on Tuesday, April 13, 1742. Public interest was so great that ladies were asked to come without hoops to their dresses and gentlemen without swords, so that 700 people could be fitted in instead of the usual 600. The chorus was drawn from the cathedral choirs of Christ Church and St Patrick's and the composer himself was at the harpsichord. The work was received with great enthusiasm and one of the Dublin newspapers described it as "the finest composition of music that ever was heard". The proceeds were divided between

three Dublin charities, Mercer's Hospital, the Infirmary on Inn's Quay, and the prisoners in the various jails. Handel was always happy to help those less fortunate than himself.

He wrote several more fine oratorios and religious works, but *Messiah* holds a unique place not only in his output but in the whole of musical literature. Its strength and directness speak even to those whose knowledge of music is limited. This work, written by a German living in England for an Irish audience, has a universality that rises above all the accidental

Interior of the Church of Oberammergau, South Germany, the village where the famous Passion Play is performed every tenth year. The church was built about 1740 and is a fine example of the Rococo style.

boundaries of time and place.

After the deaths of Bach and Handel, musical interest moved from Lutheran Germany to Catholic Austria. The second half of the eighteenth century was dominated by Joseph Haydn (1732-1809) and Wolfgang Amadeus Mozart (1756-1791), who worked mainly in and around Vienna and gave us the type of Mass which is often called the Viennese Mass. This was very different from the polyphonic Mass of the time of Palestrina. In addition to a choir, it involved solo singers and an orchestra and it was written in the same style as music written for the concert hall or the opera house.

This is particularly true of Mozart's Masses, which are charming and elegant but without any great depth of religious feeling. The lovely motet *Ave Verum* and the Requiem Mass written towards the end of his short life are more spiritual than his earlier works and show how his music might have developed had he lived. He was actually working on the Requiem during his last illness and the knowledge that he would never live to finish it must have given it its unusual poignancy.

Haydn was twenty-four years older than Mozart but outlived him by eighteen years. During the last years of his life he devoted himself almost entirely to religious music. Between 1796 and 1802 he wrote two oratorios, *The Creation* and *The Seasons,* and six Masses, all of them ranking among his greatest works. *The Creation* was supposed to be based upon Milton's *Paradise Lost* but Haydn, one of the most cheerful and likeable of men, decided to leave out any reference to such depressing topics as Satan, hell and sin. The result is one of the most delightful and lighthearted of all oratorios, a hymn to the innocent beauty of the newly created world.

The prevailing mood of the last six Masses is also one of joy but those critics who have called them shallow are mistaken. The easy flow of the music comes from very careful construction and the choruses have a strength and simplicity that is worthy of Handel at his best. Haydn's faith in God was childlike and untroubled and he showed this in his compositions. "When I think of God, my heart leaps with joy", he told a friend, "and I cannot help my music doing the same."

The same qualities are to be found in the Catholic churches built in Austria and south Germany around this time, the most important contribution to church architecture made in the eighteenth century. They were built in a style which is sometimes called Late

Baroque and sometimes Rococo, a style of almost unrestrained joy and gaiety. These churches are plain on the outside but inside they are aswirl with colour and movement and light. Altars and pulpits are twisted into fantastic shapes, walls appear to curve and sway, marble pillars with gilded capitals point the way to the painted ceilings, where crowds of angels and saints soar ecstatically among the clouds.

The first impression made by one of these churches is a little overpowering, but a closer examination shows how skilfully they are constructed. Architects such as Balthasar Neumann (1687-1753) were masters of design and knew how to balance the elaborate decorations with areas of plain white wall and large clear windows. The same criticisms have been made of Neumann as of Haydn, that his art is shallow and frivolous and unworthy of something as serious as religion. It is true that both of them stress one side of religion, the joyful side, but they do it so happily and skilfully that one has to admire and enjoy the result.

Joseph Haydn died in 1809. As he lay dying in his home in Vienna, Napoleon's troops were capturing the city and the ancient monarchies of Europe were collapsing on every side. The Age of Revolution had come.

CHAPTER SEVEN

THE AGE OF REVOLUTION

The French Revolution, which threw all Europe into turmoil from 1789 on, came to an end with Napoleon's defeat at Waterloo in 1815. The kings were put back on their thrones, even in France. After a quarter of a century of revolutions and republics, everything was the same as it always had been.

Yet nothing was really the same any more. The kings were back, but they had been overthrown once and everyone knew that they could be overthrown again. The nineteenth century was to see a long series of revolutions all over Europe which were to strip the kings bit by bit of their power and transfer it to the people. It was the century during which power passed from the aristocracy to the middle class, though not yet to the working class.

Christianity did not come to an end. Indeed it was stronger in the nineteenth century than it had been in the eighteenth. The Deism of Voltaire and his followers was forgotten and middle-class religion took its place. Sometimes it was hypocritical, sometimes it was puritanical, especially in matters of sexual morality, but it was founded on a firm and sincere faith. The visionary poet and painter, William Blake (1757-1827), lived to see the transition:

Mock on, mock on, Voltaire, Rousseau:
Mock on, mock on: 'tis all in vain!
You throw the sand against the wind,
And the wind blows it back again.

And every sand becomes a gem
Reflected in the beams divine;
Blown back they blind the mocking eye,
But still in Israel's paths they shine.

The atoms of Democritus
And Newton's particles of light
Are sands upon the Red Sea shore,
Where Israel's tents do shine so bright.

William Blake.

The religious problems of the nineteenth century were problems for the Church rather than for Christianity. Churchmen failed to see that the passing of the old monarchies was a liberation for the Church. They had been so accustomed to the close link between

Church and Crown that they felt threatened by the coming of democracy. This led to difficulties in many countries, especially in Italy, where the Pope in 1871 was deprived of the Papal States and left a virtual prisoner in the Vatican.

It was only in Ireland, under the leadership of Daniel O'Connell (1775-1847), that the Church was clearly on the side of democracy and opposed to the remnants of royal despotism. It was because of the backing of the people of Ireland that O'Connell won Catholic Emancipation in 1829, not only for the Catholics of Ireland but for those of Britain as well. If he failed in his further aim of securing Home Rule for Ireland, it was only because he was not prepared to plunge his country into violence and bloodshed to achieve his end.

Daniel O'Connell.

Emancipation meant an official end to the persecution under which the Catholics of both countries had suffered for 300 years. In Ireland, where the vast majority of people were Catholics, it was now possible for them to live a fully Catholic life and to replace their mean chapels with handsome new churches. The Irish religious orders which had been founded to educate the young, such as the Christian Brothers and the Presentation Sisters, could expand freely and other orders were started to assist in the work. Irish priests and brothers and nuns also began to go abroad as missionaries throughout the English-speaking world: to Britain, to the United States, to Australia and New Zealand, to the British colonies scattered all over Africa and Asia.

Cardinal Newman

After the defeat of Napoleon, England dominated Europe and the world. The religious life of England was dominated by one man, John Henry Newman (1801-1890), whose long lifetime spanned almost the whole of the century. He spent the first half of that life as an Anglican and the second as a Catholic, and his influence on both Churches was and still is profound.

Cardinal Newman.

He first became well-known as the leader of the Oxford Movement. This was the name given to a group of young Anglicans at Oxford University who were trying to reform the Church of England and make it less Protestant. They believed that the Anglican Church was part of the Catholic Church and that it occupied the middle ground between the two extremes of Protestantism and Romanism. Newman and his friends tried to bring back many of the things that had been swept away by the Protestant Reformation:

143

Interior of University Church, Dublin. In 1854 Newman commissioned J.H. Pollen to design it in the Byzantine style, as he did not favour the Gothic style.

devotion to the saints, prayers for the dead, an unmarried clergy, a greater use of ceremonies and vestments in worship, a deeper respect for the sacraments and especially for the eucharist. For the first time ever a bridge was beginning to be built between Catholics and Protestants and Newman was the chief bridge-builder.

The Oxford Movement caused a storm of opposition in the Church of England. Newman was accused of being a secret Roman Catholic and he resigned his post as vicar of St Mary's Anglican Church in Oxford. He went to live in the nearby village of Littlemore and there began work on a very important book which he called *An Essay on the Development of Christian Doctrine.* It looked at the whole history of religion and showed how Christians had reached a fuller understanding of many of Christ's teachings through centuries of prayer and reflection. By the time he had finished the book, he himself had come to the most important decision of his life.

He sent for an Italian priest who was in the neighbourhood. The priest arrived late at night, soaked to the skin by pouring rain. "I took up my position by the fire to dry myself," he wrote later. "The door opened — and what a spectacle it was for me to see at my feet John Henry Newman begging me to hear his confession and admit him into the bosom of the Catholic Church! And there by the fire he began his general confession with extraordinary humility and devotion." The following day he received Newman and some of his companions into the Catholic Church. It was October 9, 1845.

It was the end of Newman's doubts but only the beginning of his troubles. He had to leave his beloved Oxford and live in the ugly industrial town of Birmingham. He had to endure savage attacks by many Protestants, who said it proved that he had been a secret Roman Catholic all the time. He had to endure suspicion from many Catholics, who thought he was still a Protestant at heart. When he went to Rome to be ordained priest, he found that the theologians there did not approve of his books. Back in Birmingham, he was unjustly sued for libel and lost the case. He went to Dublin in 1854 to be rector of the new Catholic University there but resigned after three years because of difficulties with the Irish bishops. A magazine he was editing was attacked by the English bishops and criticised by the Pope. Everything he did seemed to turn out badly. "I have no friend at Rome," he wrote in his journal, "I have laboured in England, to be misrepresented, backbitten and scorned. I have laboured in Ireland, with a door ever shut in my face."

Gerard Manley Hopkins as a youth.

Towards the end of 1863 a wellknown Anglican clergyman and author, Charles Kingsley, wrote a review for a magazine which included these words: "Truth, for its own sake, has never been a virtue with the Roman clergy. Father Newman informs us that it need not, and on the whole ought not to be." It was a polite way of saying that Catholic priests in general and Newman in particular were liars. Newman asked in vain for an apology from Kingsley. Then he decided that he could only end the attacks on his sincerity by writing a history of his religious opinions and telling the reasons which brought him to the leadership of the Oxford Movement and then to the Church of Rome. He called the book *Apologia Pro Vita Sua* (A Defence of his Life).

He began the *Apologia* in mid-April and finished it on June 12, 1864. It was published in instalments, a chapter every week. Despite his age (he was 63) he worked for up to sixteen hours a day on the book, standing at a tall writing-desk; once he wrote for twenty-two hours without a break. A man waited at the door of the room to take the pages to the printers as soon as they were finished.

It is not the rushed and careless work one might

Interior of St Aidan's Cathedral, Enniscorthy, Co. Wexford, by Pugin. The altar area was re-modelled after the Second Vatican Council to fit in with the liturgical changes.

expect under the circumstances. It is one of the masterpieces of Christian literature, and its fascinating combination of theology and autobiography makes it worthy to stand beside St Augustine's *Confessions*. The passage in which he speaks of the Catholic doctrine of original sin shows the masterly way in which he marshals his thoughts and the beautiful style in which he expresses them:

> To consider the world in its length and breadth, its various history, the many races of man, their starts, their fortunes, their mutual alienation, their conflicts; and then their ways, habits, governments, forms of worship; their enterprises, their aimless courses, their random achievements and acquirements, the impotent conclusion of long-standing facts, the tokens so faint and broken of a superintending design, the blind evolution of what turn out to be great powers or truths, the progress of things, as if from unreasoning elements, not towards final causes, the greatness and littleness of man, his far-reaching aims, his short duration, the curtain hung over his futurity, the disappointments of life, the defeat of good, the success of evil, physical pain, mental anguish, the prevalence and intensity of sin, the pervading idolatries, the corruptions, the dreary hopeless irreligion, that condition of the whole race, so fearfully yet exactly described in the Apostle's words, "having no hope and without God in the world" — all this is a vision to dizzy and appal, and inflicts upon the mind the sense of a profound

mystery, which is absolutely beyond human solution.

What shall be said to this heart-piercing, reason-bewildering fact? I can only answer, that either there is no Creator, or this living society of men is in a true sense discarded from his presence. Did I see a boy of good make and mind, with the tokens on him of a refined nature, cast upon the world without provision, unable to say whence he came, his birthplace or his family connections, I should conclude that there was some mystery connected with his history, and that he was one of whom from one cause or other his parents were ashamed. Thus only should I be able to account for the contrast between the promise and condition of his being. And so I argue about the world; — *if* there be a God, *since* there is a God, the human race is implicated in some terrible aboriginal calamity. It is out of joint with the purposes of its Creator. This is a fact, a fact as true as the fact of its existence; and thus the doctrine of what is theologically called original sin becomes to me almost as certain as that the world exists, and as the existence of God.

Newman's *Apologia* was an instantaneous success. The honesty and anguish of the book convinced

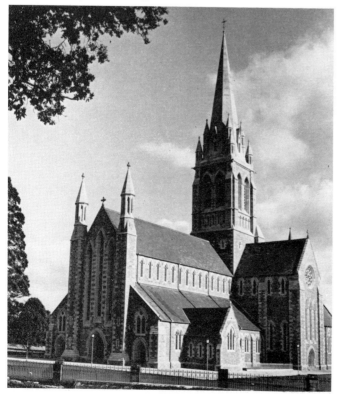

St Mary's Cathedral, Killarney, by Pugin. According to his son this noble building was Pugin's favourite among all the churches he designed.

The Light of the World by Holman Hunt, which shows Christ knocking at the door of the soul. When asked why there was no handle on the door, the artist replied that it could only be opened from the inside.

fair-minded Protestants that he was utterly sincere in his beliefs. In Rome Pius IX remained suspicious to the end but his successor, Leo XIII, made Newman a Cardinal in 1879. "The cloud is lifted from me for ever," said the old man gratefully. He lived another ten years and was close to 90 when he died, mourned by Catholics and Protestants alike.

He had given Protestants a new appreciation of the sacraments, of the dignity of worship, of the importance of tradition in the life of the Church. He had taught Catholics to respect the views of others and to recognise that truth itself does not change but our understanding of it does. He had inspired the pioneers of the movement for reunion among Christians. He had laid the foundations for the Second Vatican Council. He was certainly a great man and possibly a saint.

Of all his many friends and disciples, there is space to mention only one. Gerard Manley Hopkins (1844-1889) was a student at Oxford when the *Apologia* was published and he was deeply impressed by it. He went to Birmingham to see Newman and was received by him into the Catholic Church. He then decided to join the Jesuit Order, which had been re-established in 1814 after its long suppression. He was ordained priest in 1877 and in 1884 became Professor of Classics at Newman's University in Dublin. He died there in 1889 and was buried in Glasnevin Cemetery.

Only a few close friends knew that he wrote poems in his spare time. None of the poems was published during his lifetime. After his death they began to circulate and appear in print but a complete edition was not published until 1918. It was only then that he came to be recognised as one of the most original and sensitive of all the Victorian poets.

One poem begins with the words: "The world is charged with the grandeur of God." That was the theme of all his poetry: the hand of God visible in the world he has created. Hopkins saw beauty in the smallest and most unexpected things. His notebooks have drawings of twigs and buds, his poems pick out odd details such as the flash of tinfoil or the colours of oozing oil or the patterns in the mud of a country laneway. In his poem *Pied Beauty* he gives thanks for everything "counter, original, spare, strange"; and the same adjectives could be applied to his own verses:

Glory be to God for dappled things—
For skies of couple-colour as a brinded cow;
For rose-moles all in stipple upon trout that swim;

Fresh firecoal chestnut-falls; finches' wings;
Landscapes plotted and pieced — fold, fallow, and
plough;
And all trades, their gear and tackle and trim.

All things counter, original, spare, strange;
Whatever is fickle, freckled (who knows how?)
With swift, slow; sweet, sour; adazzle, dim;
He fathers-forth whose beauty is past change:

Praise him.

Hopkins never sought recognition or complained at
its absence. Like the birds and the weeds and the
wildflowers, his poems went on praising God whether
men looked at them or not.

The Gothic Revival

"He has the great fault of a man of genius, as well as
the merit. He is intolerant and, if I might use a strong
word, a bigot." Thus did Newman describe another
famous English convert of the nineteenth century. He
was right. Augustus Welby Pugin (1812-1852) was
both a genius and a bigot; but today his intolerance is
forgotten and the fruits of his genius remain.

Pugin became a Catholic in 1835, at the age of
twenty-three. It was his interest in Gothic architecture
that led to his conversion. "I assure you," he wrote to a
friend, "that after a most close and impartial
investigation, I feel perfectly convinced that the
Roman Catholic Church is the only true one, and the
only one in which the grand and sublime style of

Christ in the House of his Parents
by Sir John Everett Millais
(1829-1896). The boy Jesus has
cut his hand on a nail and is being
comforted by his mother.

Two typical "holy pictures". Mawkish pictures of this kind were very popular in the nineteenth century and are still sometimes to be found today.

architecture can ever be restored." The rest of his life was devoted to restoring the grand and sublime style which he believed could only be found in the buildings of the Middle Ages.

Architecture at this time was in a state of confusion. The Baroque style was now fallen out of fashion, though the more classical style of Wren still had its followers. Others went further back into history and produced buildings in the Renaissance style, in the Gothic style, in the Roman style, in the Greek style, even in the style of ancient Egypt. "It is not the expression of existing opinions and circumstances," wrote Pugin, "but a confused jumble of styles and symbols borrowed from all nations and periods." He even attacked those who claimed to be using the Gothic style for their shoddy buildings and their mock-mediaeval furniture:

All the ordinary articles of furniture, which require to be simple and convenient, are made not only very expensive but very uneasy. We find diminutive flying buttresses about an armchair; everything is crocketed with angular projections, innumerable mitres, sharp ornaments, and turreted extremities. A man who remains for any length of time in a modern Gothic room, and escapes without being wounded by some of its minutiae, may consider himself extremely fortunate.

In book after book Pugin lacerated the enemies of art, among whom he included the Protestant religion. "The degraded state of the arts in this country," he said, "is purely owing to the absence of Catholic feeling among its professors, the loss of ecclesiastical patronage, and the apathy with which a Protestant nation must necessarily treat the higher branches of art." He was just as hard on those Catholics (such as Newman) who preferred Renaissance to Gothic churches, or Mozart to Gregorian Chant, or who did not agree with him that the altar should be separated from the congregation by a rood-screen. He had tremendous rows, he wrote blistering letters, he burst into floods of tears, he went off in a sulk and sailed around in an old fishing boat for weeks at a time. In the end, he usually got his way.

His most famous building is the Houses of Parliament in London, which he worked on in collaboration with another architect, Sir Charles Barry. He also designed many of the churches that the Catholics of Britain began to build in the years

St Thérèse, photographed by her sister Céline. In spite of the cross and the lilies, the saint's face shows both humour and shrewdness.

following emancipation. In England these included cathedrals at Southwark (later destroyed in an air-raid), Birmingham, Newcastle and Nottingham, as well as various parish churches.

Some of his finest work was done in Ireland. He designed the strong stark cathedral at Killarney and the more graceful one at Enniscorthy, along with convents, colleges, and parish churches. He worked at tremendous speed and did all his own drawing. When asked why he did not employ a clerk to help him he gave the reasonable reply: "A clerk? I should kill him in a week." In the event, it was himself that he killed. His over-worked brain gave way and he was only 40 when he died.

In addition to the churches he designed himself, he set a standard for church building that was followed by many other architects. The fine nineteenth-century Gothic churches found throughout Ireland and England and in many other countries owe their inspiration to him. He has also influenced the whole course of modern architecture by his writings, particularly his book *The True Principles of Pointed or Christian Architecture:*

The two great rules for design are these: first, that there should be no features about a building which are not necessary for convenience, construction, or propriety; second, that all ornament should consist

151

of enrichment of the essential construction of the building.

These two principles were new at the time but today all architects would accept them. They would also accept two other rules he laid down: that "construction should vary with the material employed" and that "the external and internal appearance of an edifice should be illustrative of and consistent with the purpose for which it is destined". It was a plea for honesty in architecture: that stone should be treated like stone, that a church should look like a church, that the most straightforward solution to a problem was generally the best one. The Gothic Revival is now a thing of the past but Pugin's principles still apply with as much force as ever in the modern world of steel girders and pre-stressed concrete.

Hearts and Flowers

During the nineteenth century, religious art continued to decline and became steadily more feeble and sentimental. A few efforts were made to improve the situation but they did not meet with any lasting success. A group of German artists who were nicknamed the Nazarenes worked in Rome during the early years of the century and tried to revive religious art by modelling their work on the best paintings of Raphael and his predecessors; they produced some good but not outstanding pictures.

A similar group was formed in England in 1849 which believed that even Raphael was a little too smooth and professional. They wanted to recapture the innocence and attention to detail of the painters before Raphael and so they called themselves the Pre-Raphaelite Brotherhood. Though they did not confine themselves to religious subjects, they painted many

St Thérèse after death, painted by her sister Céline. The artist has succeeded in removing every trace of personality from Thérèse's face.

152

scenes from the Bible and from Christian history and literature. One of the best known of the Pre-Raphaelites, William Holman Hunt (1827-1910), paid several visits to the Holy Land in order to make the background to his biblical scenes as accurate as possible.

Archaeology became an aid to inspiration and sometimes a substitute for it. Other artists made the journey to the Hóly Land, among them the Frenchman James Tissot (1836-1902), who lived there for ten years and produced a remarkable series of paintings of the Old Testament and of the life of Christ. Every single detail in them was carefully researched and they come nearer than any previous pictures to what the reality must have been like. But they do not have the artistic power of the great painters of the period 1300 to 1700. These Old Masters did not care about historical accuracy and were quite happy to use the clothing and houses and landscape of Italy in their biblical scenes; but they conveyed the spiritual meaning of these happenings in a way that Tissot could never attain.

This did not prevent artists like Hunt and Tissot from becoming very popular. They gave the public what they wanted and the public they reached was a very large one, thanks to developments in the technique of printing pictures. Middle class drawingrooms had books illustrated by Tissot on their occasional tables, engravings of Hunt's *The Light of the World* or Millais's *Christ in the House of his Parents* on

153

their walls. The middle classes knew little about art but they knew what they liked: pictures which told a story and made a direct appeal to the emotions.

The second half of the century saw religious art at its lowest point, sentimental and effeminate. What were called "holy pictures" were painted by untalented and anonymous artists and manufactured in huge numbers, large-sized for hanging on the wall or small-sized for putting in the prayer book. The main characteristics of these pictures are still all too familiar: the effeminate Christ, the doll-faced Madonna, the curly-haired Child Jesus, the simpering angels and saints, all swimming in a soup of clouds and doves and hearts and flowers. Plaster statues of the same type were made for the home and for the church and painted in garish colours. Many fine church buildings were and some still are disfigured by crude plaster images of the Sacred Heart, our Lady of Lourdes, and various popular saints. Works of religious art were no longer commissioned from the artist's studio but were bought ready-made from the repository, the name given to the religious goods shop. It has been called the period of repository art.

While lamenting this shoddy and sentimental art, we must not forget that many people drew strength and inspiration from it. It is not necessary to be a good art critic in order to be a good Christian. An outstanding instance of this is St Thérèse of Lisieux (1873-1897), who was completely typical of her time and of her narrow provincial upbringing, yet became one of the most influential figures of nineteenth-century Christianity.

Thérèse Martin was the youngest of five girls in a respectable middle-class family, who lived in the small

Left:
Franz Liszt, dressed as a priest.

Right:
Giuseppe Verdi.

town of Lisieux in northern France. All five became
nuns, four of them in the Carmelite Convent at
Lisieux. Thérèse entered there at the unusually young
age of fifteen and took the name Sister Thérèse of the
Child Jesus. Nine years later she died of tuberculosis,
not yet 25 years old. During the last years of her life
she was asked by her superiors to write an account of
her life and this was published shortly after her death.
Almost overnight the unknown young nun became
world-famous, innumerable favours and miracles were
attributed to her intercession, and in 1925 she was
canonised.

In her *Autobiography* Thérèse compared herself to a
little flower and that rather sugary title has clung to her
ever since. The pictures of her painted by her sister
Céline, a competent artist, are equally sugary. A typical
one shows the saint laid out after her death, crowned
with roses and surrounded by flowers, while an angel
with a flaming arrow, feebly imitated from Bernini,
peers from behind a curtain. Even the photographs
which Céline took of her follow the same pattern:
Thérèse standing with her arms around the foot of the
cross, Therese kneeling with a spray of lilies in her
hands.

Yet this Little Flower was made of steel. Her way to
God was no primrose path, it was not marked by
visions or raptures. It lay in the daily battle to
overcome her failings and to keep cheerful in all her
trials, both great and small. In this excerpt she tells the
Reverend Mother about one such battle:

Sir Edward Elgar.

> For a long time, at evening prayers, my place was
> just in front of a sister who had an odd nervous
> affection; I expect she had a lot of lights, too, in her
> prayer, because she hardly ever used a book. What
> made me notice she was rather odd was that the
> moment she came in she began to make a curious
> little noise, rather like what one would make by
> rubbing two shells together. Nobody noticed it
> except me; but then I've got a very sensitive ear —
> perhaps too sensitive on some occasions. I simply
> can't describe to you, Mother, how that tiny noise
> got me down. I longed to turn round and give the
> offender one look; obviously she was quite
> unconscious of fidgeting, and it didn't seem as if
> there was any other way to let her know about it. But
> something told me — something deep down inside
> me — that the right thing to do was to put up with it
> for the love of God, and spare the sister any
> embarrassment.

The Troitse-Sergieva Monastery, Moscow, founded in the 14th century. After the fall of Constantinople, the Byzantine tradition of art and architecture was carried on by the Russian Orthodox Church.

So I stayed still, and tried to get closer to God; perhaps I could forget it altogether, this tiny noise. Absolutely useless; there was I with the sweat pouring down me, in the attempt to make my prayer into a prayer of mere suffering! Suffering — but somehow I must get rid of the nervous irritation, and suffer peaceably, joyously; that is, with peace and joy deep down in my soul. So I hit on the idea of trying to *like* this exasperating noise, instead of trying vainly not to hear it. I devoted myself to listening hard, as if the sound were that of some delightful music, and all my prayer — it certainly wasn't the prayer of quiet! — consisted in offering this music to our Lord.

The last years of her life saw her trials increasing. In addition to the burden of her illness, she had to go through the dark night of the soul in the form of severe temptations against her faith. "All right, all right, go on longing for death!" said the voice of doubt. "But death will make nonsense of your hopes; it will mean a night darker than ever, the night of mere non-existence."

Dear Mother, does it sound as if I were exaggerating my symptoms? Of course, to judge by the sentiments I express in all the nice little poems I've made up during the last year, you might imagine that my soul was as full of consolations as it could hold; that for me the veil which hides the unseen hardly existed. And all the time it isn't just a veil, it's a great wall which reaches up to the sky and blots out the stars! No, when I write poems about the happiness of heaven and the eternal possession of God, it strikes no chord of happiness in my own heart — I'm simply talking about what I'd determined to believe. Sometimes, it's true, a tiny ray of light pierces through the darkness, and then just for a moment the ordeal is over; but immediately the memory of it brings me no happiness, it seems to make the darkness thicker than ever.

Mother, I don't think I'd ever quite realised before how gracious and merciful God is to us; he sent me this ordeal just when I was strong enough to bear it — earlier on, I might well have given way to discouragement, whereas now it only serves to purge away all that natural satisfaction which my longing for heaven might have brought me. Dear Mother, what's left now to hinder my soul from taking its flight? The only thing I want badly now is to go on loving till I die of love.

Beneath the hearts and flowers was a truly great soul. Her writings and her example have led many other souls to God by showing them that holiness does not consist in doing extraordinary things but rather in doing ordinary things extraordinarily well.

Mass and Oratorio

It was in the field of music that the nineteenth century made its greatest contribution to the Christian heritage. Between Beethoven's *Christ on the Mount of Olives* (1800) and Elgar's *The Dream of Gerontius* (1900) a majestic series of masterpieces gave expression to the religious beliefs of the great composers of the time. It is possible to mention only a few of them here.

In the Catholic countries almost every composer wrote at least one setting of the Mass and many wrote oratorios and motets as well. Ludwig van Beethoven (1770-1827) spent almost five years on his great *Missa Solemnis* (Solemn Mass) which was originally intended for a church ceremony but grew longer and longer as the composer poured all his deepest feelings into its composition. Finished at last in 1823, it was recognised

Fyodor Dostoievsky.

as a sublime and truly spiritual work; but it was too long to be used in church and the composer himself agreed that it was more suited for the concert hall. The same problem was to arise many more times during the century, since composers were now writing in a much more expansive style than that of the eighteenth century and even their symphonies and concertos were twice as long as those of their predecessors. It is often difficult to judge whether some of these nineteenth century Masses were meant to be church works or concert oratorios.

This is not to question the sincerity of the men who composed them. Most of them were genuinely religious men, sometimes to the point of eccentricity. Franz Liszt (1811-1886) had a rather disreputable youth but became very pious in later years, composed many religious works, received minor orders, dressed like a priest, and liked to be called "the Abbé Liszt". Anton Bruckner (1824-1896) used to interrupt his lectures at the Vienna Conservatory when the Angelus bell rang and kneel down to say his prayers. His nine symphonies were as religious in feeling as his three Masses; his last symphony was dedicated to God.

A preoccupation with death was a mark of many composers of this time, as is shown by the number of settings of the *Requiem* Mass, the Mass for the Dead. The erratic Frenchman, Hector Berlioz (1803-1869) wrote a famous *Grande Messe des Morts* (Grand Mass for the Dead) which required a choir of at least two hundred voices, an immense orchestra, sixteen kettledrums, and four separate brass bands at the four corners of the church. The *Requiem* of Giuseppe Verdi (1813-1901) is in the dramatic style one would expect from the composer of so many operas and has become one of the most popular of all his works; its most famous section is the *Dies Irae,* which conjures up the terrible day of judgment in an overwhelming avalanche of sound. Other composers adopted a more gentle approach to the mystery of death. The lovely *Requiem* of Gabriel Fauré (1845-1924) is tender and trusting in mood and leaves out the *Dies Irae* sequence altogether. The *German Requiem* written by the Lutheran Johannes Brahms (1833-1897) is not a setting of the Latin Mass at all but of a number of texts from the Bible; the music is a serene message of Christian hope in the face of death.

The Protestant countries, and England in particular, continued to cultivate the oratorio. The popularity of Handel's *Messiah,* the advance in musical education, the availability of cheap printed scores, all contributed to the growth of amateur choirs and choral societies throughout the country. Music festivals were organised at which old favourites were revived and new works given a hearing. The most important of these was the Birmingham Festival, held every three years, at which many important oratorios were given their first performance.

The first work to rival *Messiah* in popularity was Mendelssohn's *Elijah*, which had its premiere at Birmingham in 1846. Felix Mendelssohn (1809-1847) was as popular in England as in his native Germany, and his sentimental *Songs Without Words* were played by every amateur pianist in the country, including the Prince Consort himself. His oratorio tells the dramatic story of the prophet Elijah and is filled with picturesque incidents: Elijah's cure of the widow's son, his contest with the priests of Baal, his vision of God in the still small voice, his ascent to heaven in a fiery chariot. The music is descriptive and appealing, with touching solo arias and massive choruses. It is almost too appealing: like much of Mendelssohn's music, it is a little superficial and sentimental. These qualities endeared the work to Victorian audiences but are less attractive to the audiences of today.

The Birmingham Festival continued to sponsor new works by leading composers of the time, both British and foreign. Mendelssohn was a Lutheran but Charles Gounod *(The Redemption* in 1882 and *Mors et Vita* in 1885) and Antonin Dvorak *(Requiem* in 1891) were Catholics. A large number of oratorios by English composers were also given their premieres but none of them met with lasting success: they had all the faults of Mendelssohn without his virtues. Among them was Arthur Sullivan who thought that his oratorio *The Light of the World* (Birmingham 1873) and other similar works would make him immortal. He was greatly frustrated when the public preferred the charming but lightweight music he wrote as part of the famous Gilbert and Sullivan partnership.

It was not until the very end of the century that an Englishman wrote a great oratorio. *The Dream of Gerontius* by Edward Elgar (1857-1934) had its premiere at the Birmingham Festival of 1900. It was given a cool reception for reasons that were religious rather than musical; the composer was not only a Catholic but seemed to have gone out of his way to offend Protestant feelings. The work, based on a poem by Cardinal Newman, told of the death and judgment of Gerontius and was filled with references to Catholic beliefs and practices: quotations from the Latin liturgy, prayers for the dead, invocations of our Lady and the saints. The end was the worst of all, with an angel leading Gerontius to Purgatory and leaving him with these words:

> Angels, to whom the willing task is given,
>   Shall tend and nurse and lull thee as thou liest;
> And Masses on the earth and prayers in heaven
>   Shall aid thee at the Throne of the Most Highest.

> Farewell, but not for ever, brother dear,
>   Be brave and patient on thy bed of sorrow;
> Swiftly shall pass thy night of trial here
>   And I will come and wake thee on the morrow.

"It stinks of incense," said one indignant critic. It took many years before it was given the recognition it deserved.

The Dream of Gerontius is divided into two parts; within each part the music flows continuously and is not broken up into separate numbers as in the older oratorios. The short and intense first part describes the death of Gerontius and ends with a magnificent chorus based on the prayers of the Roman Ritual: "Go, in the name of angels and archangels!" The second part follows the journey of the soul after death through a grotesque chorus of demons, a radiant hymn from the angelic hosts, and a series of mighty orchestral chords as the soul approaches the Judgment Seat. The angel's leavetaking at the end is set to one of the most meltingly beautiful of all Elgar's melodies. When he had finished the composition, the composer wrote on the score, "This is the best of me." Prophetic words, for he never again reached the same height of inspiration.

The Voice of Russia

The middle classes looked at pictures, listened to music, and above all read novels. The nineteenth century was the age of the great novelists. In the absence of radio and television, people had plenty of time for reading and they were in no hurry to get to the end of the story. The average novel of the period was three or four times as long as the modern novel.

Most of the novelists reflected Christian beliefs in their works, if only to avoid offending their readers, but these beliefs were not often given much prominence. The immensely successful Charles Dickens, for instance, used religion mainly as a way of squeezing a few extra drops of sentiment out of the

Leo Tolstoy, dressed as a Russian peasant and carrying a Bible in his pocket.

The Glorification of St Ignatius of Loyola by Andrea Pozzo (1642-1709), on the ceiling of the Church of St Ignatius, Rome. Pozzo was a Jesuit lay brother and the greatest master of this kind of aerial perspective.

Stained glass window in Eton College Chapel, England, by Evie Hone. The upper part of the window depicts the Crucifixion, and the lower part shows the Last Supper with the sacrifice of Melchisedek on the left and the sacrifice of Abraham on the right.

many death scenes that occurred in his books. It was mainly in the works of the great Russian novelists that religion became an important and even dominant theme.

The entry of Russia into European affairs was one of the most striking events of the century. It began with Napoleon's invasion of Russia in 1812, which put an end to centuries of Russian isolation. The Russia which was now opened up was a strange and backward country, a police state in which the Czar wielded absolute power and the peasants lived in grinding poverty and near-slavery. Napoleon's invasion was unsuccessful but the revolutionary ideas he brought with him remained on after him. The huge country began to rumble with discontent against its corrupt and tyrannical rulers.

Among the revolutionaries was a young writer named Fyodor Dostoievsky (1821-1881). In 1849 he was arrested in St Petersburg and sentenced to death. He was standing in front of the firing squad when a messenger arrived to say that his sentence had been changed to penal servitude. After ten years in Siberia he was allowed back to St Petersburg and resumed his career as a writer.

In view of the ghastly ordeal he had gone through, it is not surprising that the balance of his mind was affected and that he began to suffer from epileptic fits. It is not surprising either that guilt and redemption became the major themes in his writings. His first important novel was called *Crime and Punishment* and it told the story of a student who brutally murdered an old woman. It was only by admitting his guilt and accepting his sentence that he finally achieved peace of mind.

His last and greatest novel was *The Brothers Karamazov*. It tells of a young man who is found guilty of murder, this time falsely, but who accepts his sentence as punishment for his other sins. What gives the novel its special quality is the way its events are examined in the light of Christianity; and for western readers there is the added interest that it is Russian Christianity, the faith of the Orthodox Church that had lost contact with the West for almost a thousand years. The saintly old monk, Father Zossima, is a key figure in the book and it is he who expresses its central message:

My friends, pray to God for gladness. Be glad as children, as the birds of heaven. And let not the sin of men confound you in your doings. Fear not that it

161

will wear away your work and hinder its being accomplished. Do not say: 'Sin is mighty, wickedness is mighty, evil environment is mighty, and we are lonely and helpless and evil environment is wearing us away and hindering our good work from being done.'

Fly from that dejection, children. There is only one means of salvation. Then take yourself and make yourself responsible for all men's sins. That is the truth, you know, friends, for as soon as you sincerely make yourself responsible for everything and for all men, you will see at once that it is really so and that you are to blame for everyone and for all things. But throwing your own indolence and impotence on others, you will end by sharing the pride of Satan and murmuring against God.

The voice of eastern spirituality echoes through this book and through all of Dostoievsky's works, the voice that had not been heard in the West since the days when the sayings of the Desert Fathers were read in the monasteries of the first Benedictines.

The other great Russian novelist, Leo Tolstoy (1828-1910), was a nobleman and landowner who was concerned with problems of justice rather than problems of guilt. His two great novels are *War and Peace* and *Anna Karenina*. The first of these is an epic story of the Russian struggle against Napoleon, in which the author tries to find some meaning behind all the suffering and misery that war brings to mankind. *Anna Karenina* is on a somewhat smaller scale and describes the tragedy of a married woman who falls in love with another man. Anna's unhappiness is contrasted with the happiness of a young landowner, Levin, whose return to his religion ends the book:

'This new feeling has not changed me, made me happy, enlightened me all at once; it is rather like the first feeling that I had for my son. It did not take me by surprise either. Through suffering it has entered my heart imperceptibly, and taken up its abode there. I shall probably get angry with Ivan the coachman the same as ever, embark upon useless discussions, express my thoughts irrelevantly just as before. There will always be the same dead wall between my soul and that of others, even with my wife; I shall probably go on accusing her in my anxiety and repenting of it afterwards. I shall continue to pray without being able to explain to myself why. But my life, my whole life,

Leo XIII being carried in procession through the Sistine Chapel.

independently of what may happen to me, every minute of it, shall no longer be senseless as before, but every moment, every action shall be invested with meaning.'

Levin is a self-portrait of Tolstoy. The doubts which troubled him in *War and Peace* were solved in the writing of *Anna Karenina*. From then on the Gospels were his guide and companion and he tried to put their teaching into effect in his life, though as he grew older his understanding of them became more and more unusual. He no longer believed literally that Christ was God or that he rose from the dead, but he did take literally the command to sell one's goods and give to the poor. He gave away all his property to his relatives and began to live and work among the poorest peasants. His wife objected to this and he had many violent quarrels with her during the last years of his life. After one such quarrel, the 82-year-old Tolstoy decided to leave her secretly; he was taken ill on the train and died in a room in a small country railway station, besieged by journalists and cameramen from

163

all over the world. The Russian Orthodox Church declared that he had been guilty of heresy and refused him Christian burial.

Dostoievsky and Tolstoy not only wrote the most powerful novels of the nineteenth century, they also foreshadowed the problems of the twentieth. It was in Russia that these problems existed in their most acute form: tyranny, inequality, poverty. Tragically, when the Russian revolution came in 1917 it was not the peaceful Christian one that these writers had hoped for but a revolution of hate and violence. It replaced a corrupt and tyrannous government ruling in the name of God by a corrupt and tyrannous government ruling in the name of the people.

There was another man who saw these problems and hoped for a Christian solution. That was Leo XIII, who was Pope from 1878 to 1903. The First Vatican Council of 1870 had declared the infallibility of the Pope and Leo used the added authority this gave him by writing encyclical letters on the main problems of the day. Though these letters were not intended as infallible statements, they were received with considerable respect both inside and outside the Church. The most notable of them was *Rerum Novarum,* dealing with the condition of the working classes.

It was not only in Russia that the poor were oppressed. The peasants of Western Europe still lived on the verge of starvation, as was tragically proved by the terrible Irish famine of 1847 during which more than a million people died. Those who left the land to find work in the new industrial towns did not greatly improve their lot. The middle classes lived comfortably, the upper classes luxuriously, but the workers had barely enough to stay alive. "A small number of very rich men," said Pope Leo, "have been able to lay upon the teeming masses of the labouring poor a yoke little better than that of slavery itself." He went on:

At the time being, the condition of the working classes is the pressing question of the hour; and nothing can be of higher interest to all classes of the State than that it should be rightly and reasonably settled. But it will be easy for Christian working-men to solve it aright if they will form associations, choose wise guides, and follow on the path which was trodden by their fathers before them with so much advantage to themselves and to the common good. Prejudice, it is true, is mighty, and so is greed for money; but if the sense of right and justice is not deliberately stifled, their fellow citizens are sure to be won over to a kindly feeling towards men whom they see to be in earnest as regards their work and who prefer so unmistakably right dealing to mere lucre and the sacredness of duty to every other consideration.

The Pope's appeal on behalf of the rights of workers and particularly his approval of workers' associations (that is, trade unions) made a powerful impression at the time. The fact that social change came through peaceful means in most countries is due in no small measure to the wisdom and concern of Leo XIII.

CHAPTER EIGHT

THE TWENTIETH CENTURY

Leo XIII died in 1903 and was succeeded by St Pius X, the only Pope to be canonised in the last four hundred years. He took as his motto *Instaurare Omnia in Christo* (To restore all things in Christ) and his aim was to make sure that the spiritual and artistic treasures of the Christian tradition should not be lost to the twentieth-century Church.

One of his first acts was to issue a *Motu Proprio* or Instruction on sacred music. French Benedictines had produced new and more accurate editions of the Gregorian Chant melodies and German scholars had rediscovered and published many of the works of the sixteenth-century composers. The *Motu Proprio* encouraged the use of Gregorian Chant and classical polyphony in church and particularly at Mass and discouraged the more operatic and flamboyant styles of music. It led to a great improvement in standards of church music all over the Catholic world.

Equally important was the Decree on Frequent Communion of 1905. Scholars pointed out that in the early centuries Christians had normally received Holy Communion whenever they attended Mass. It was only in the Middle Ages that people had begun to hold back through excessive reverence, and this false attitude had been strengthened later on by the influence of Jansenism. Pius X went back to the earlier tradition and recommended that Catholics receive Communion frequently and even daily, as long as they did so worthily and with the right intentions.

In the field of philosophy and theology, Pius X followed in the footsteps of Leo XIII by holding up Thomas Aquinas as an example of a great Christian thinker. As a result of this, the writings of St Thomas were taught and studied more widely and were found to be much less out-dated than people had imagined. A renewed form of St Thomas's philosophy, called Thomism, was developed by some of the most eminent thinkers of the time.

The Defeat of Modernism
One of the most significant of Pius X's actions was the condemnation of Modernism. In 1907 he issued an encyclical letter in which he pointed out some dangerous mistakes being made by certain Catholic

writers, and he gave the name "Modernism" to the viewpoint they were expressing.

Modernism, like Jansenism, was more an attitude than a heresy. It sprang from a praiseworthy desire to keep the lines of communication open between the Church and the sciences. Ever since Darwin had published his book *The Origin of Species* (1859), it had become clear that the story of Creation in the Bible could not be taken as a literal account of the origin of the world. Increased knowledge of history had also shown that many Christian beliefs and practices appeared to have altered in the course of the centuries.

Fifteen years before Darwin's book, Newman had dealt with some of these problems in his book *The Development of Christian Doctrine*. After his death, followers of Newman carried his theories further; in some cases, they carried them too far. They seemed to be suggesting that there was nothing in the Bible or in the teaching of the Church that was absolutely true, and indeed that truth itself was changing all the time.

Charles Darwin.

Right:
Pierre Teilhard de Chardin.

This is what Pius X meant by Modernism. He did not attack any writers by name but he did warn about the errors into which they were falling or likely to fall. Among the errors he condemned were the following:

> Truth is not unchangeable any more than man is, since it evolves with him and in him and through him.
>
> ⋆
>
> Christ did not teach a definite body of doctrine applicable to all times and to all men, but rather started a kind of religious movement which has to be adapted to different times and places.
>
> ⋆
>
> Present-day Catholicism cannot be reconciled with true science unless it is transformed into a kind of non-dogmatic Christianity, that is, into broad and liberal Protestantism.

In addition to censuring these and other similar propositions, the Pope ordered that all priests should take an oath rejecting Modernism. Most priests and indeed most Catholics accepted all this without question. When Pius X died in 1914 the defeat of Modernism was complete.

In a way, the defeat of Modernism was too complete. Unknown to the Pope, the battle against the Modernists had turned into a witch hunt. Fanatical anti-Modernists formed themselves into a sort of secret society with its headquarters in Rome and contacts in many countries. They threw accusations of Modernism around wildly, they spread rumours, they blackened characters, they wrote anonymous letters, they published libellous articles under false names. The new Pope, Benedict XV (1914-1922) tried to clear the air but without much success. A heavy atmosphere of suspicion hung over all Catholic thinkers and they were liable to be accused of heresy if they showed any

Church at Raincy, France, by Perret. The architect did not use any of the styles of the past but created a new style of his own for this church.

St Michael by Epstein. This bronze group shows the Archangel Michael victorious over Satan and is attached to the outside of Coventry Cathedral, England.

interest in modern ideas or in the advances of science.

One of the victims of this suspicion was a French Jesuit, Pierre Teilhard de Chardin (1881-1955). Teilhard was a scientist as well as a priest, an expert in palaeontology, the study of ancient forms of life. As a palaeontologist, he worked in many parts of the world, including China and Africa, digging up the fossils that

revealed the early history of the human race. His studies convinced him that man had indeed evolved from lower forms of life, as Darwin said. But neither Darwin nor any other scientist had explained why this evolution had taken place.

Teilhard found the explanation in what he called love, the force that links all thinking beings, that draws

Interior of Coventry Cathedral. The altar is dominated by an immense tapestry designed by Graham Sutherland, which shows Christ in majesty surrounded by the symbols of the four evangelists.

171

men towards one another and towards God. According to his theory, love is the force which moves through all created things, rocks and plants and animals as well as men. It is the force which makes them evolve from lower to higher forms and which draws the human race on towards the last stage of evolution. This last stage is reached when all mankind is completely united together and made perfect; Teilhard called this stage the Omega point, because Omega is the last letter of the Greek alphabet. What will man be like when he has reached the Omega point? He will be like Jesus Christ, said Teilhard, the most perfect of men and the destination towards whom all evolution is moving.

The most striking thing about Teilhard's theory is that it is based on scientific reasoning. He does not try to bring religion and science together as two separate things. He tries to show that religion and science are inseparable and that the line of reasoning which begins with the fossilised remains of early man ends with the vision of Christ, in whom the whole universe finds fulfilment. It is possible to pick holes in some parts of his philosophy but it still remains a brilliant and profound attempt to answer the fundamental questions of modern science.

Teilhard explained his theories in a number of books, the most important of which is *The Phenomenon of Man,* written between 1938 and 1940. Unfortunately, his religious superiors suspected him of leaning towards Modernism. They allowed him to study but not to teach. They allowed him to write books but not to publish them. He accepted this calmly and humbly as is shown by a letter he wrote in 1951 to the Jesuit General in Rome:

> I can truly say — and this in virtue of the whole structure of my thought — that I now feel more indissolubly bound to the hierarchical Church and to the Christ of the Gospel than ever before in my life. Never has Christ seemed to me more real, more personal or more immense.
>
> How then can I believe that there is any evil in the road I am following?
>
> I fully recognise, of course, that Rome may have its own reasons for judging that in its present form my concept of Christianity may be premature or incomplete and that at the present moment its wider diffusion may therefore be inopportune.
>
> It is on this important point of formal loyalty and obedience that I am particularly anxious — it is in fact my real reason for writing this letter — to assure

Right:
Church at Dublin airport by Robinson, Keeffe and Devane. The courtyard in front of the church provides an area where people can meet and talk after Mass.

Interior of Parish Church, Dun Laoghaire, Co. Dublin, by Pearse McKenna. The sanctuary is in accordance with recent liturgical directives and shows (left to right) the tabernacle pillar, the ambo and the high altar. Art work by Michael Biggs and Enda King.

you that in spite of any apparent evidence to the contrary, I am resolved to remain a child of obedience ...

Let me repeat that, as I see it, this letter is simply an exposition of conscience and calls for no answer from you. Look on it simply as a proof that you can count on me unreservedly to work for the Kingdom of God, which is the one thing I keep before my eyes and the one goal to which science leads me.

After his death in 1955 his friends began to publish the books that have since made him famous. It is sad that Teilhard was no longer there to profit by the discussion they provoked and to develop and amend his theories as a result. It is sad that for fifty years religion and science had been let drift into an attitude of opposition while the man best fitted to prevent this was silenced.

Teilhard was not the only one to suffer in this way. There were other Catholic thinkers who had to endure the same suspicion and opposition. The first half of the twentieth century saw a great missionary expansion of the Church in Africa and Asia, but it also saw a loss of Christian influence among educated and scientific circles in Europe and America.

New Pathways in Art

The years from 1914 to 1918 were the years of World

War 1. People called in the Great War at the time, not knowing that there was a greater one to come. World War II lasted from 1939 to 1945. The upheavals caused by these wars was no doubt one reason for the decline in the arts which took place in the twentieth century, though there were other reasons as well. Religious art did not escape the general decline altogether, but it did have some successes to its credit.

Church architecture was one field in which a real advance took place. By 1900 or so the Gothic Revival had run out of steam and designers of churches were once again thumbing through the pages of history books in search of inspiration. The new cathedral at Westminster in England was being built in the old Byzantine style. Irish architects were using the Irish Romanesque style, based on the twelfth-century Cormac's Chapel at Cashel. Some of these churches were good of their kind but the better architects were beginning to feel unhappy at the idea of delving into the past for designs and ignoring the new building methods which were coming in, especially the use of reinforced concrete.

The First World War put a stop to all church building and it was not until 1923 that the first modern church was opened for divine worship. It was the church of Notre Dame de Raincy near Paris and it was designed by the French architect Auguste Perret (1874-1954). It was built of reinforced concrete and made no attempt to hide the fact: even the marks left by the wooden casing into which the concrete had been poured were still visible. The ground plan was conventional — a rectangle with pillars and aisles — but the appearance of the completed church was unlike any church ever seen before and it opened the eyes of architects to all kinds of new possibilities.

Between the wars, a small number of modern churches were built in different countries, among them an unusual diamond shaped church at Turner's Cross, Cork. After World War II, the number of these new-style churches increased sharply, especially in Germany, where many churches had been destroyed by air-raids. Pillars were no longer needed to support the roof with new building methods so pillars were abandoned. The rectangular shape and the cross shape were also abandoned in many instances as architects tried to work out the relationship between the altar and the congregation. Experiments were made with different shapes as in the Baroque era but for a different reason. The Baroque architects were interested in making buildings which would be

175

Igor Stravinsky.

beautiful and interesting to look at; the modern
architects were interested in making buildings in which
people could pray more easily and take their proper
part in divine worship. The altar was brought nearer
the congregation and in some cases was made into a
free-standing table so that the priest could face the
people while saying Mass.

Modern artists were employed to decorate the
modern churches. Most artists at this time were
suffering from what might be called a communication
problem. Art had become abstract and inward-looking
and was no longer understood by the man in the street.
The artist working for the church had to make a special
effort to be clear and to produce a recognisable image.
This may be the reason why religious art in recent
times has often been high in quality though small in
quantity.

The French painter Georges Rouault (1871-1958) is
probably the greatest of the modern religious artists.
He began his career as a designer of stained glass
windows and this early training influenced his
paintings. He expressed his religious emotions most
strongly in the many paintings and etchings he made of
his favourite subject, the Passion of Christ. Many of
these look like stained glass, with rich colours

T.S. Eliot.

separated by heavy black lines like the lead between the different coloured panes in a church window. Compared to a nineteenth-century religious painting his work seems crude and even brutal, but this helps him to portray the pain and desolation of Christ in a way that was beyond the power of the smooth Victorian artists.

In England the sculptor Jacob Epstein (1880-1959) and the painter Graham Sutherland (born 1903) are among the leading names in recent religious art. Both of them contributed works to the new Anglican cathedral at Coventry, one of the landmarks of post-war church building. Ireland's most important contribution has been in stained glass. The windows of Michael Healy (1873-1941) have a noble simplicity while those of Harry Clarke (1889-1931) are brilliant and sparkling. The stained glass work of Evie Hone (1894-1955) shows the influence of Rouault and has great strength and depth of feeling; her window in Eton College, England, is a modern masterpiece, fully worthy of its mediaeval setting. There has also been a notable flowering of Irish religious architecture and sculpture and metalwork, so that recent Irish churches rank among the finest in the world in design and ornamentation.

The situation in regard to music is not so happy. Early in this century composers began to grow weary of the modes or keys which had governed melody and harmony from the very beginning of written music. Audiences were unable to follow them as they experimented with 12-note scales and other seemingly arbitrary methods of composition. Communication between the serious composer and the public has been growing more difficult since the nineteen-twenties and has now reached almost complete breakdown.

This process can be seen at work in the career of the great Russian composer, Igor Stravinsky (1882-1971), whose later compositions are much less popular than his earlier ones. A devout Christian, he lived in exile from Russia after the revolution and transferred his allegiance from the Orthodox to the Catholic Church. His Latin *Mass* (1948) is an austere and somewhat forbidding work in comparison with his earlier *Symphony of Psalms* (1930). This Symphony, which he described as "composed to the glory of God", is a setting for chorus and orchestra of three psalms and is one of his loveliest and most easily understood works.

None of the works of the French composer Olivier Messiaen (born 1908) is easily understood but he is unquestionably one of the most significant of living composers. As well as being a writer and teacher of music, he is organist of a church in Paris and his music is deeply religious in inspiration. The names of some of his principal works read like a litany: *The Apparition of the Eternal Church, Quartet for the end of time, Twenty looks at the infant Jesus, The transfiguration of our Lord Jesus Christ,* and so on. Present day listeners find his music intriguing but baffling; it remains to be seen whether it will communicate more easily with listeners in the future.

The Convert Writes

It is a surprising fact that almost all the great Christian literature of the twentieth century has been written by converts. It may be that the experience of conversion brings an appreciation of the Christian values which those who have known them from their cradle take for granted.

The most important voice in Christian literature in the first half of the century was that of T.S. Eliot (1888-1965). He was born in America but moved to England in 1914 and spent the rest of his life there. More significant was the spiritual journey which led him from agnosticism into the Church of England in 1927. His Anglican faith, very close to Catholicism in

G.K. Chesterton.

all essentials, became the inspiration of all his later poems and plays.

Eliot is not an easy poet to read. The difficulty does not lie in the words he uses, which are simple to the point of flatness: he deliberately avoids poetical language and his verse often sounds like prose. The difficulty lies in the thought behind the words. Even when one has tracked down all the countless references to ancient and modern literature, the meaning often remains unclear.

Yet even when the meaning is hidden, his poems make a powerful impression on the mind. In his earlier works, the impression is one of sadness and unfulfilled longing:

> I grow old . . . I grow old . . .
> I shall wear the bottoms of my trousers rolled.
> Shall I part my hair behind? Do I dare to eat a
> peach?
> I shall wear white flannel trousers, and walk upon
> the beach.

Graham Greene.

I have heard the mermaids singing, each to each.
I do not think that they will sing to me.

In *The Hollow Men,* dated 1925, the poet's soul
seems to be torn between pagan despair and Christian
hope. Parodies of nursery rhymes and snatches of
prayers break in on the debate and at times reduce it
almost to incoherence:

Here we go round the prickly pear
Prickly pear prickly pear
Here we go round the prickly pear
At five o'clock in the morning.

Between the idea
And the reality
Between the motion
And the act
Falls the Shadow
                              For Thine is the Kingdom

Evelyn Waugh.

Between the conception
And the creation
Between the emotion
And the response
Falls the Shadow
                    Life is very long

Between the desire
And the spasm
Between the potency
And the existence
Between the essence
And the descent
Falls the Shadow
                    For Thine is the Kingdom

For Thine is
Life is
For Thine is the

This is the way the world ends
This is the way the world ends
This is the way the world ends
Not with a bang but a whimper.

181

Alexander Solzhenitsyn.

His later poems, particularly the haunting *Four Quartets,* are marvellous meditations on the meaning of human existence. The pain is still there but its cause has now been identified. It is the pain that the soul must suffer as long as it is in exile from its true home.

> You say I am repeating
> Something I have said before. I shall say it again.
> Shall I say it again? In order to arrive there,
> To arrive where you are, to get from where you are not,
> You must go by a way wherein there is no ecstasy.
> In order to arrive at what you do not know
> You must go by a way which is the way of ignorance.
> In order to possess what you do not possess
> You must go by the way of dispossession.
> In order to arrive at what you are not
> You must go through the way in which you are not.
> And what you do not know is the only thing you know.
> And what you own is what you do not own
> And where you are is where you are not.

It is almost word for word the message of St John of the Cross. The pain of this world is the pathway to God.

The novel grew shorter and declined in importance in the present century as people turned to other forms of entertainment. But there were still some writers who found in the novel a way of examining Christian truth and among them three English novelists are worthy of mention, all of them converts to the Catholic Church. They are G.K. Chesterton, Evelyn Waugh and Graham Greene.

Gilbert Keith Chesterton (1874-1936) was more than a novelist. He was a journalist, an essayist, a poet and, in the best sense of the word, a personality. He attacked the enemies of Christianity with a good humour that endeared him even to those he was attacking. He is remembered by most people for his detective stories, in which the amiable Father Brown unravels mysteries and unmasks murderers, while making some telling theological points along the way. But his poems, essays, books of philosophy and theology, social and literary criticism, lives of saints, and many other works do not deserve to be forgotten: they say some very profound things in a lighthearted manner.

Evelyn Waugh (1903-1966) was as scathing as Chesterton was genial. His early novels were satirical studies of England's godless rich, savage and heartless and wildly funny. As an army officer during World War II, he witnessed the ruthless Communist take-over in Eastern Europe and his post-war novels are more serious in tone, beginning with *Brideshead Revisited* which described, as he said himself, "the operation of divine grace on a group of diverse but closely connected characters."

The last years of his life were devoted mainly to the massive *Sword of Honour*. This is a sequence of three novels about the Second World War as seen through the eyes of an English officer who, like Waugh himself, is a crusty conservative Catholic with a barely controlled loathing for the modern world and all it stands for. It is difficult to sympathise with some of Waugh's views but the wit and style with which he expresses them are irresistible.

The operation of divine grace is a central theme in most of the writings of Graham Greene (born 1904). He divides his books into novels (serious works) and entertainments (thrillers) but the division is not very clear-cut; his novels are gripping stories, his entertainments have unexpected depths. His best work is probably to be found in two novels he wrote in the nineteen-forties. *The Power and the Glory* is a story of a hunted priest in anticlerical Mexico; the human weaknesses of the whiskey priest make the light of grace shine all the more clearly in his life. *The Heart of the Matter* is set in West Africa and tells of a Catholic colonial officer who is led by human sympathy into sin: first the sin of adultery and then the sin which is in theory unforgivable, suicide. But the compassionate ending of the novel suggests that no sin is unforgivable in the sight of God.

None of these novelists attained or tried to attain the epic scale of the great nineteenth-century Russian novelists. But in Russia itself, in a country where all the power of a police-state was used to spread atheism and to discredit religion, two Christian novelists emerged to carry on the tradition of Tolstoy and Dostoievsky.

Boris Pasternak (1890-1960) was born of Jewish parents but was converted to Orthodox Christianity some time between the wars. Though well-known as a poet, he was fortunate enough to escape the imprisonment or death that befell most of Russia's best writers under Stalin. After World War II he began work on a vast novel describing the life of a Russian doctor-poet in the years between 1901 and 1929, the years that saw the wheel go full circle from Czarist tyranny to Stalinist tyranny. The novel took ten years to write and was named after its hero, *Doctor Zhivago*.

As long as Stalin lived, there could be no hope of publishing *Doctor Zhivago*. The book told both sides of the story and did not conceal the fact that the rulers of Communist Russia had betrayed the ideals to which they paid lip-service. The old brutality and terror still went on under new management. In addition, the book included a number of very beautiful poems, most of them on Christian themes, which were supposed to have been written by Zhivago but were of course by Pasternak himself. In 1955, however, Stalin was dead and the new rulers were promising greater freedom. Pasternak submitted his novel for publication. It was turned down by the censors.

A copy of the manuscript had been sent to Italy before the censors stepped in. It was translated and published in many languages and greeted all over the world as the greatest novel to come out of Russia since the death of Tolstoy. Pasternak was awarded the Nobel Prize in 1958 but was prevented by the Soviet government from accepting it. He became the target of a campaign of slander and abuse which only ended in his death in 1960. His request to be given a Christian burial was refused.

Pasternak soon found a worthy successor. Alexander Solzhenitsyn was born in 1918 and given the usual atheist education of the period. He served with distinction in the Red Army during World War II until early 1945, when he was suddenly arrested and accused of criticising Stalin in letters to friends. He was sentenced to eight years' penal servitude for this crime. After his release he began writing and in 1962 managed to get his short novel about the forced labour camps *One Day in the Life of Ivan Denisovitch* published in Moscow. It is said that Khrushchev himself authorised its publication as part of his shortlived campaign for de-Stalinisation. The book caused an immense sensation in Russia and throughout the world as an authentic and moving account of the life lived by millions of political prisoners under Stalin's rule.

Meanwhile Solzhenitsyn was working on a large-scale novel called *The First Circle* (the title refers to Dante's *Inferno*) and dealing with life in a special category prison. The novel included a very unflattering portrayal of Stalin himself and looked critically at many aspects of Soviet life apart from the prison system. It also spoke with unaccustomed sympathy about the Church, since some time previous to this Solzhenitsyn had become a Christian.

> 'What makes you think the Church is being persecuted?' Yakonov protested. 'Nobody stops them ringing their bells, baking their communion bread, holding their Easter processions — as long as they keep out of civic affairs and education.'
>
> 'Of course they're persecuted,' Agnia protested in her usual low voice. 'If people are allowed to say and write what they like about the Church without it being able to answer back, if church valuables are confiscated and priests banished — isn't that persecution?'
>
> 'Have you seen any priests being banished?'
>
> 'That's not the sort of thing you see on the street.'
>
> 'And what if it is being persecuted?' Yakonov challenged her. 'What are ten years, when the Church was the persecutor for ten centuries?'
>
> 'That was before my time.' Agnia shrugged her thin shoulders. 'I only know what happened in my own lifetime.'

Pope John XXIII at the opening of the Second Vatican Council.

The First Circle was turned down by the censors. So was another important novel, *Cancer Ward*. So were several short stories, including *The Easter Procession*, an account of a religious procession in Moscow trying to push its way through crowds of jeering teenagers. But they were published and acclaimed in the West and in 1970 the author was awarded the Nobel Prize. He was at once subjected to the same persecution as Pasternak, but he was a younger and stronger man and he did not die. He was by now so well-known throughout the world that the Soviet authorities were afraid to imprison him although they had imprisoned several of his fellow authors. So in 1974 they expelled him from the Soviet Union.

The novels of Pasternak and Solzhenitsyn do not make altogether easy reading. They are long and slow-moving by present-day western standards. Their religious message is veiled because of the circumstances under which they were written. But they are a magnificent witness to the power of Christianity to survive and to ennoble and a prophetic warning of what will happen to a nation which turns its back on God.

Pope John's Revolution

The pontificates of Pius XI (1922-1939) and Pius XII

185

(1939-1958) were overshadowed by Nazism and Communism. Hitler's pagan empire was defeated in 1945 but not before it had taken the lives of most of Europe's Jews and many of its leading Christians.

The German Lutheran pastor Dietrich Bonhoeffer (1906-1945) was arrested in 1943 for his opposition to Hitler and executed in 1945. His last writings, published later as *Letters and Papers from Prison*, examined the place of Christianity in a world which seemed to have lost faith in religion and thought it could answer all its problems without God. Towards the end of 1944 he began to plan a book on the subject and wrote to a friend about it:

> I am enclosing the outline of a book I have planned. I don't know whether you will be able to make anything of it, but I believe you already have some idea of what I am driving at. I only hope I shall be given the peace and strength to finish it.
>
> The Church must get out of her stagnation. We must move out again into the open air of intellectual discussion with the world, and risk shocking people if we are to cut any ice. I feel obliged to tackle this question myself as one who, though a "modern" theologian, is still aware of the debt we owe to liberal theology. There will not be many of the younger men who combine both trends in themselves.
>
> What a lot I could do with your help! But even when we have talked things over and clarified our minds, we still need to pray, for it is only in the spirit of prayer that a work like this can be begun and carried through.

He never lived to write the book but his approach was to influence many others, Catholics as well as Protestants. Indeed, one effect of Hitler's persecution was to bring Christians closer together. Bonhoeffer himself conducted a service for Catholic and Protestant prisoners on the day before his death and the same kind of thing happened in many other camps and prisons. It was time for Christians to forget their differences and go to meet a world which was moving away from all forms of Christianity.

The man who finally brought the Church to meet the modern world was Pope John XXIII (1958-1963). Born in 1881 of Italian peasant parents, he spent much of his life in the diplomatic service of the Church and met people of many religions and of no religion. He was almost 77 years of age when elected Pope and no one expected him to live very long or do very much. There was general amazement when he announced that

The Last Supper from Cecil B. DeMille's **King of Kings**. The part of Christ was played by H.B. Warner.

he intended to hold a general council of the Church and fixed the date for the autumn of 1962. Since the Council of Trent in the sixteenth century, there had been only one attempt to hold a general council and that not very successful: the Vatican Council of 1870 had been prevented from completing its work by the fall of Rome.

On October 11, 1962 Pope John opened the Second Vatican Council. His opening speech marked the direction in which he wished the Council to move, a direction which had already been indicated in some of the speeches and writings of Pius XII. Pope John disowned those whom he called "the prophets of doom", the people who thought the world was sunk in sin and almost beyond redemption. He asked the Council not to issue condemnations but to bring to humanity once again the true teaching of Jesus Christ, restated in the light of modern scholarship and in the language of modern man. "The substance of the ancient deposit of faith is one thing," he said, "the way in which it is expressed is another." Finally, he called for a coming together in unity not only among all Christians but among the followers of all religions.

John XXIII died in 1963 but the Council continued on under Paul VI until 1965. The various documents issued by the Council make up a volume of 700 pages and they are important not only for what they say but for where they point. The Church has since advanced in many cases beyond the guidelines laid down by Vatican II. But without those guidelines the later advances would not have been possible.

The most obvious change was the phasing out of Latin as the customary language of worship. Many Catholics regretted this but it was hard to defend the use of a language which was no longer spoken anywhere in the world. The task now facing the Church is to realise that a whole new idea of worship is involved. It is not just the change from one language to another: it is the change from quiet presence to active participation and it poses problems for both priest and people.

One problem is the restructuring of churches to suit the new liturgy. The older churches were built for a liturgy in which the priest was remote and detached from the people and it is difficult to adapt them for a liturgy of participation without spoiling their beauty as architecture; the moving of the altar may upset the whole design of the church. Another problem is finding music for the new words. The only composers who are able to reach an audience today are the composers of popular music and so it is not surprising that Folk Masses in the pop music style have come into favour, especially among young people. It would be a great loss, however, if the settings of the Latin rite, whether Gregorian Chant or harmonised music, were to fall into disuse.

The ecumenical movement, the movement for religious unity, has continued to gain ground. The visit of the Archbishop of Canterbury, the leader of the Anglican Church, to Pope John was a step of great significance; so was the meeting in Jerusalem between Pope Paul and the head of the Orthodox Church, Patriarch Athenagoras. Joint services, discouraged before the time of Pope John, have become so frequent that people are asking what the next step is. Complete Christian unity is not yet in sight but the movement towards it has been more rapid than anyone could have expected in 1958.

A quite unexpected development which has taken place since Vatican II is the movement known as Pentecostalism or the Charismatic Renewal. This is a prayer movement which started among some Catholics at Duquesne University, Pittsburgh, in 1967 and spread quickly to other parts of the U.S.A. and then around the world. Groups of people meet together in one another's houses to pray together and to allow the Holy Spirit to work in their souls. They not only find

Moses leading the people of Israel out of Egypt. Artist's design for one of the most spectacular of all film sequences, from DeMille's 1956 version of **The Ten Commandments.**

peace and spiritual renewal at these meetings but feel they have been granted special charisms or gifts, such as speaking in unknown tongues, interpreting the scriptures, powers of healing and exorcism, charisms which are mentioned in the New Testament though they seem to have vanished later from the main stream of Christian life. In any event, the importance of the Charismatic Renewal Movement does not depend on the genuineness or otherwise of these charisms but on the way it has helped many people to a deeper life of prayer and a greater understanding of the Bible. Its prayer meetings also serve in many places as a bridge between Christians of different denominations.

For older Catholics, Vatican II has been an unsettling experience. They feel the Church has changed too much and changed too quickly. Their feeling is understandable. Change is always difficult and when it has been long delayed it can easily go out of control. Pope John's revolution was needed because the Church had become too inward-looking and too backward-looking, but there is now the danger that Christians may go too far in the opposite direction and abandon some of their most precious possessions in the name of progress. It is not easy to have a moderate revolution.

The Christian Heritage

Never before have so many people lived on this earth as in the last quarter of the twentieth century. Never before has material progress been so rapid, technology so advanced or education so widespread. Yet the

189

artistic achievements of our century do not compare favourably with those of previous ages.

One new art has been developed since 1900, the art of the cinema. *The Great Train Robbery* (1903) was the first film to tell a continuous story, *The Jazz Singer* (1927) was the first one to have synchronised speech, *Becky Sharp* (1935) was the first feature in full colour. Since then, further technical advances have been made, including wide-screen photography and stereophonic sound; but cinema audiences have fallen off since the end of World War II and the coming of television.

Christianity has shown itself in the cinema in two main ways. The first is by the use of themes from the Bible or from Church history as subjects for films, often with huge amounts of money spent on spectacular settings, costumes and special effects. The great master of this type of film was the Hollywood director Cecil B. DeMille (1881-1959). His films were more popular with the public than with the critics. "I am sometimes accused of gingering up the Bible with lavish infusions of sex and violence," he once said, "but I wish that my accusers would read their Bibles more closely, for in those pages are more sex and violence than I could ever portray on the screen." In spite of this rather one-sided view of the Bible, there are moments of real religious power in such films as *The King of Kings* (1927), *The Sign of the Cross* (1932), *Samson and Delilah* (1949) and *The Ten Commandments* (1956). But the main appeal of these films and their many imitators has little enough to do with Christianity.

The other way is seen in films which look at everyday life in the light of Christian belief. Here again the results have been disappointing. Most of these films are sentimental and unreal, with false problems set up so that they can be solved for a happy ending. This technique is seen at its best in a film like Leo McCarey's *Going My Way* (1944), beautifully acted and directed, highly enjoyable but with little resemblance to actual life.

One of the few directors who have tried to ask and answer honest questions is Sweden's Ingmar Bergman (born 1918). The son of a Lutheran pastor, Bergman in his earlier films was concerned with the pain of living and the difficulty of making contact with God. Sometimes he set his stories in the Middle Ages, as in *The Seventh Seal* (1956) and *The Virgin Spring* (1960), two of his finest films. In *Winter Light* (1961) and *Through a Glass Darkly* (1962) the scene is set in modern Sweden, where God seems to be much farther away. Bergman's later films seem to have abandoned the search for religious meaning; they are still honest and expertly made but they chill the heart.

If Augustus Welby Pugin were alive today, he would no doubt explain it all by saying that art must die unless it is nourished by religion. He would point to the triviality and unimportance of present-day films and plays. He would compare the beauty of even the humblest modern church with the soulless inhumanity of the great office blocks that are filling our cities. He would mention the modest success of much recent religious painting and sculpture and stained glass work in contrast with similar work of a non-religious nature. He would say that Solzhenitsyn towers above his contemporaries not because he is a greater writer but because he believes more passionately in the things he writes. It is obviously an oversimplification to say, as Pugin once did say, that the degradation of the arts is due to the absence of Catholic feeling. Nevertheless, the connection between art and religion has always been a close one. Even before the time of Christianity, the first beginnings of art were inspired by religious feelings. People become poets and painters and musicians because they believe there is more to life than living. They try to create beauty because they believe that there is such a thing as beauty. When people cease to believe in anything apart from themselves, they lose part of their humanity.

Alexander Solzhenitsyn was born and·bred in the world's first completely godless civilisation. His prose poem *A Journey Along the Oka* says all that needs to be said about a land which has been robbed of its Christian heritage.

Travelling along country roads in Central Russia you begin to understand why the Russian countryside has such a soothing effect.

It is because of its churches. They rise over ridge and hillside, descending towards wide rivers like red and white princesses, towering above the thatch and wooden huts of everyday life with their slender, carved and fretted belfries; from far away they greet each other; from distant unseen villages they rise towards the same sky.

Wherever you wander, over field or pasture, many miles from any homestead, you are never alone: above the wall of trees, above the hayricks, even above the very curve of the earth itself, the dome of a belfry is always beckoning to you, from Borki

Lovetskie, Lyubichi or Gavrilovskoe.

But as soon as you enter a village you realise that the churches which welcomed you from afar are no longer living. Their crosses have long since been bent or broken off; the dome with its peeling paint reveals its rusty rib-cage; weeds grow on the roofs and in the cracks of the walls; the cemetery is hardly ever cared for, its crosses have been knocked over and its graves ransacked; the ikons behind the altar have faded from a decade of rain and are scrawled with obscene graffiti.

In the porch there are barrels of salt and a tractor is swinging round towards them, or a lorry is backing up to the vestry door to collect some sacks. In one church machine-tools are humming away; another stands silent, simply locked up. Others have been turned into clubs where they hold propaganda meetings ("We Will Achieve High Yields Of Milk!") or show films: "Poem about the Sea", "The Great Adventure".

People have always been selfish and often evil. But the angelus used to toll and its echo would float over village, field and wood. It reminded man that he must abandon his trivial earthly çares and give up one hour of his thoughts to life eternal. The tolling of the eventide bell, which now survives for us only in a popular song, raised man above the level of a beast.

Our ancestors put their best into these stones and these belfries — all their knowledge and all their faith.

Come on, Vitka, buck up and stop feeling sorry for yourself. The film starts at six, and the dance is at eight. . . .